Strange Fruit

THE BIOGRAPHY
OF A SONG

THE ECCO PRESS
An Imprint of HarperCollins*Publishers*

Strange Fruit

David Margolick

Foreword by Hilton Als

HarperCollins books may be purchased for educational, business, or sales promotional use. For information please write: Special Markets Department, HarperCollins Publishers, Inc., 10 East 53rd Street, New York, NY 10022.

FIRST EDITION

Designed by Cassandra J. Pappas

Library of Congress Cataloging-in-Publication Data

Margolick, David.
Strange fruit: the biography of a song / David Margolick.
—1st ed.
p.   cm.
Originally published: Philadelphia: Running Press, © 2000.
Discography
ISBN 0-06-095956-8
1. Allan, Lewis, 1903–1986.   Strange fruit.   2. Holiday, Billie, 1915–1959—Political and social views.   3. Lynching—Southern States—Songs and music—History and criticism.   4. Protest songs—United States—History and criticism.   I. Title.

ML3551.M29 2001
782.42165—dc21
00-047688
01 02 03 04 05   RRD   10 9 8 7 6 5 4 3

To the City of New York,

which gave "Strange Fruit"—and me—a home

Acknowledgments

THIS BOOK was not only a labor of love, but labor-intensive, too. I have many debts to acknowledge.

First, there are the eyewitnesses: the people who experienced "Strange Fruit" firsthand, and shared their thoughts with me: Heywood Hale Broun, Holmes "Daddy-O" Daylie, Ahmet Ertegun, Milt Gabler, Norman Granz, Lena Horne, Bernard and Honey Kassoy, Albert Murray, Max Roach, Ned Rorem, Pete Seeger, Artie Shaw, Studs Terkel, Bobby Tucker, Mal Waldron, and George Wein. There are those who've refreshed and perpetuated the song: Tori Amos, Dee Dee Bridgewater, Abbey Lincoln, Eartha Kitt, Cassandra Wilson.

Many other people assisted me. Apart from those quoted in the text, whose contributions are clearly apparent, these include Bob Adams, Jimmy Allen, Michael Anderson, George

Avakian, Charlie Bourgeois, Oscar Brand, Paul Buehl, Donald Clarke, Ron Cohen, Art D'Lugoff, William Dufty, Bill Ferris, Henry Foner, Leah Garchik, Marvin Gettleman, Farah Jasmine Griffin, John Jeremy, Ken Maley, Gertrude Margolick, David Ostwald, Carrie Rickey, Mark Satlov, Don Shirley, Chuck Stone, Elijah Wald, Jay Weston, Josh White, Jr., Douglas Yeager, and Sidney Zion. My thanks to them all.

Two of the musicians I interviewed—Harry "Sweets" Edison and Johnny Williams—died before this book was completed, and I want to pay special tribute to them, as well as to the late Jack Millar, founder and guiding light of the Billie Holiday Circle, who was unfailingly courteous to me. The book was greatly enhanced by the help and encouragement of Abel Meeropol's two sons, Michael and Robert Meeropol. I also want to thank the many people who responded to my queries about "Strange Fruit," recalling with great power and eloquence their associations with Billie Holiday, Josh White, and the song. It was a thrill to read their recollections and a privilege to include many of them in my book.

I want also to thank the incomparably knowledgeable and generous Dan Morgenstern at the Institute for Jazz Studies at Rutgers University; Tom Bourke and George Bozewick of the (also incomparable) New York Public Library; Dr. Howard Gotlieb and Sean Noel at Boston University; Peter Filardo at the Tamiment Library at New York University; Ralph Elder of the University of Texas; and Deborah Gillaspie of the Chicago Jazz Archive. The archive of my alma mater, the *New York*

Times, is another inspiring institution, and I want to thank Lou Ferrer there for his cheerful assistance.

My editors at *Vanity Fair*, Graydon Carter and Doug Stumpf, were enthused about this project from the outset, and I am grateful to them. I am thankful, too, to Buz Teacher, Caroline Tiger, Carlo DeVito, Susan Oyama, Justin Loeber, Jennifer Worick, Rebecca Helmeczi, and the many other wonderful people at Running Press who encouraged me to revisit and expand upon my research, making it an even more rewarding experience for me, and to Dan Halpern and Patricia Fernandez of Ecco Press, who have done their best to bring "Strange Fruit" and *Strange Fruit* to an even wider audience.

DAVID MARGOLICK
New York, February 2001

I've sung ["Strange Fruit"] from time to time.
You have to be careful to surround it with
some other songs; it's so powerful it brings
an audience to a dead stop.

—*Folksinger Pete Seeger*

Foreword

THERE APPEARS, in this valuable study about a significant moment in American popular music, American social life, and the distinctly American voice and presence of Miss Billie Holiday, an alarming bit of reporting. I'm trying to remember where this terrible thought first appears, so as to spare you the shock of it, but I don't want to look it up again; I found it painful enough to read the first time. I'm almost certain that it can be found twice in David Margolick's informative book, which is a large window into a small, albeit influential, world. What I'm referring to is a remark made by someone who knew Holiday. Margolick's source says something about Holiday's intelligence, pointing out that Billie Holiday, the star, did not read much in the way of "real" literature, did not have a large vocabulary, and had a fan's love of cheap romance stories about men and women who ended up on the sunny side of the street with no intimation of despair or death darkening their kisses, stories that espoused none of the terror or sarcasm or knowledge of slow death by injection with which Holiday herself infused even the happiest of her tunes, this potential candidate, we are given to understand, for Literacy Partners.

It's disgraceful—the very idea that Billie Holiday knew less than us because she reveled in what some would consider lowbrow entertainment, just as jazz was, in its time, considered lowbrow entertainment. That Holiday's preferred reading matter should be considered a reflection of her "true" self—have we not had enough of Holiday as the crude romantic primitive, a prisoner of bad lyrics, too fat or too slovenly or just too stupid to clear all those teary technicolor Modern Romance tomes off her dressing table? It's cruel, and often racist or sexist or both, to measure this definer and re-shaper of American jazz and popular singing by the mediocre standards we set for ourselves. But there we are. The Western keepers of the canon—our models of intelligence—still know so little about what makes up a Billie Holiday, let alone what makes her an authentic American female genius, a Titan in her output, that the question of her native intelligence is picked at like a scab by her detractors because she irritates them and their collective mind. Holiday makes no sense. She did not compromise her work. And she helped to create a world, a world where her voice would be at home, which is to say the world that David Margolick evokes in his seminal text about the end of New York's literal and figurative café society.

Café Society: The true home of the birth of cool, twenty years before Dizzy Gillespie and Charlie Parker donned their berets and wind instruments. It was a place that contributed greatly to the idea and reality of a New York that was, and is no longer: a city—the romantic view—that did not demand so much compromise of its artists, a city that encouraged its inhabitants to search out the substance that could be found in the stylish affect of its artists, singing and playing, some of them, in the bars and clubs of Greenwich Village, home of Holiday's voice at Café Society during a certain period in a city that is no longer.

Billie Holiday's style: It has a kind of dopey optimism, doesn't it, a kind of twisted Puritanism, the way most Negro sounds—spoken or sung or written—do, since Negroes are America, a mixture of all that we consider American: a little black, a little white, a little Native American. Her slow drawn-out sound was the sound of her time: People then took time to listen to a story, and she could tell one. I'm not sure, but I think that the first time I heard Billie Holiday's singing was the first time I realized that a singer could approximate all the bullshit and beauty that goes into a love affair. When Billie Holiday sang, she was simultaneously the embodiment of the egotism of a love affair ("Look at me! Look at me!") and a cool commentator on love's folly. And that is remarkable.

Remarkable, too, is the preservation of her myth, which Billie Holiday more than contributed to, and which David Margolick describes in his (at times) humorous and concise study. Certain questions Margolick puts to rest forever. Billie Holiday did not write "Strange Fruit," as she claimed in her unreliable but immensely readable memoir, *Lady Sings the Blues.* But she made it her own. She had so few words she could call her own, you see. And since the song became her, and she became the song, who, technically, could be called the truer auteur of "Strange Fruit"? We remember her singing the song, and we don't remember the writer, Mr. Meeropol. What does that say about the way popularity eclipses the more private environs inhabited by the writer? Would "Strange Fruit" matter to us if Billie Holiday had not sung it at a particular time, in New York, and placed all those black bodies in our minds as a way of conveying something about herself, undoubtedly, this most impersonal of biographical artists? David Margolick is interested in such philosophical questioning, and so am I.

Billie Holiday helped write the words to a number of remarkable songs, such as "Fine and Mellow" and "God Bless the Child." If you listen to them in a certain way, you'll see that they are the condensed, distinctly Negro and distinctly American version of those *True Romance* comics she read and re-read, looking for truth in something as deep and shallow as American pop, American language.

HILTON ALS

New York, November 1999

Strange Fruit

Southern trees bear a strange fruit,
Blood on the leaves and blood at the root,
Black body swinging in the Southern breeze,
Strange fruit hanging from the poplar trees.

Pastoral scene of the gallant South,
The bulging eyes and the twisted mouth,
Scent of magnolia sweet and fresh,
And the sudden smell of burning flesh!

Here is a fruit for the crows to pluck,
For the rain to gather, for the wind to suck,
For the sun to rot, for a tree to drop,
Here is a strange and bitter crop.

Southern Trees

As BILLIE HOLIDAY later told the story, a single gesture by a patron at a New York nightclub called Café Society changed the history of American music that night in early 1939, the night that she first sang "Strange Fruit."

Café Society was New York's only truly integrated nightclub, a place catering to progressive types with open minds. But Holiday was to recall that even there, she was afraid to sing this new song, a song that tackled racial hatred head-on at a time when protest music was all but unknown, and regretted it—at least momentarily—when she first did. "There wasn't even a patter of applause when I finished," she later wrote in her autobiography. "Then a lone person began to clap nervously. Then suddenly everybody was clapping."

The applause grew louder and a bit less tentative as "Strange Fruit" became a nightly ritual for Holiday, then one of her most successful records, then one of her signature songs, at least in those places where it was safe to perform. For throughout Holiday's short life—she died in 1959 at the age of forty-four—the song existed in a kind of artistic quarantine: it could travel, but only to selected places. And in the forty years since her death, audiences have continued to applaud, respect, and be moved by this disturbing ballad, unique in Holiday's oeuvre and in the repertoire of American music, as it has left its mark on generations of writers, musicians, and other listeners, both black and white, in America and throughout the world.

A "historic document," the famed songwriter E. Y. "Yip" Harburg called "Strange Fruit." The late jazz writer Leonard Feather once called "Strange Fruit" "the first significant protest in words and music, the first unmuted cry against racism." To Bobby Short, the song was "very, very pivotal," a way of moving the tragedy of lynching out of the black press and into the white consciousness. "When you think of the South and Jim Crow, you naturally think of the song, not of 'We Shall Overcome,' " said Studs

Terkel. Ahmet Ertegun, the legendary record producer, called "Strange Fruit," which Holiday first sang sixteen years before Rosa Parks refused to yield her seat on a Montgomery, Alabama, bus, "a declaration of war . . . the beginning of the civil rights movement."

Holiday performed the song countless times in her last two decades. So much about her—her appearance, her physical well-being, her personal fortunes, the sound of her voice—seemed to fluctuate wildly during that time. Though heroin and alcohol were killing her, she also experienced great moments of triumph. But whether they heard her on record or on the radio (where it was played occasionally and hesitantly by black or "nigger-loving" white disc jockeys) or got to see it performed by Holiday or someone else, those who've encountered "Strange Fruit" have found the song engraved into their consciousness. Though they may not have heard it for years, many can still recite the lyrics by heart. "Outside of knowing all of the words to 'America the Beautiful,' " a retired English professor and writer named Feenie Ziner remembered, "I don't know that there has been another song, or another singer, I could recall so completely—what is it?—sixty years later." Why? Because, as Ziner put it, "Billie Holiday tore your heart out" when she sang it. Fans of the song do not say they like it—how can one actually *like* a song on such a subject?—but they acknowledge its lasting impact. They credit it with helping awaken them to the realities of racial prejudice and the redemptive, ameliorative power of art. Whether they protested in Selma or took part in the March on Washington or spent their lives as social activists, many say that it was hearing "Strange Fruit" that triggered the process. "Would my empathy for and with the underdogs of the world have drawn me into the same career paths if I had never heard of Billie Holiday? I doubt it," said George Sinclair, a native Southerner who spent his life working with the underprivileged and disenfranchised. "If Billie Holiday didn't light the fuse, she unquestionably fed the flame."

And yet "Strange Fruit," both as a song and as a historical phenomenon, seems surprisingly unknown today. No doubt in large part because of its subject matter, it's not one of the many, many Holiday standards one encounters continually, whether on radio stations or piped in over speakers in the ubiquitous Starbucks, like "God Bless the Child," "Lover Man," "Miss Brown to You," or "I Cover the Waterfront." It is an anomaly, both inside and outside Holiday's body of work.

"Strange Fruit" defies easy musical categorization and has slipped between the cracks of academic study. It is too artsy to be folk music, too explicitly political and polemical to be jazz. Surely no song in American history has ever been so guaranteed to silence an audience or to generate such discomfort. Joe Segal has run the Jazz Showcase in Chicago, the second oldest jazz club in America, for fifty years, but he still won't listen to it when it comes on the radio. "It's too stark," he told me. "I can't handle it."

Coming out in 1939—the same year as *Gone With the Wind*, a film that embodied contemporary condescension toward blacks and black performers—and around the time that Ella Fitzgerald's "A-Tisket, A-Tasket" was more what people expected from black "girl singers"—"Strange Fruit" "put the elements of protest and resistance back at the center of contemporary black musical culture," Angela Davis wrote in *Blues Legacies and Black Feminism*. Sixty years after it was first sung, jazz musicians still speak of the song with a mixture of awe and fear. "When she recorded it, it was more than revolutionary," the drummer Max Roach said of Holiday. "She made a statement that we all felt as black folks. No one was speaking out. She became one of the fighters, this beautiful lady who could sing and make you feel things. She became a voice of black people and they loved this woman." When the song appeared, most radio stations found it too sensitive to put on the air; to this day even the most progressive disc jockeys play it only occasionally. "It's pretty intense and I'm trying to be entertaining," said Michael Bourne, who runs one of the most popular jazz programs in metropolitan New York. Those who perform the song do so almost gingerly ("It's like rubbing people's noses in their own shit," said Mal Waldron, the pianist who accompanied Holiday in her final years) and, often, only when they have to; sometimes it's just too much to take.

A few years back, *Q*, a British music publication, named "Strange Fruit" one of "ten songs that actually changed the world." Like any revolutionary act, the song initially encountered great resistance. Holiday and the black folksinger Josh White, who began performing it a few years after Holiday first did, were abused, sometimes physically, by irate nightclub patrons—"crackers" as Holiday called them. Columbia Records, Holiday's label in the late 1930s, refused to record it. And, again like revolutionary acts, the song has generated its own share of mythology, none more enduring than Holiday's oft-uttered claim that she partly wrote it herself or had it written for her. "Strange Fruit" marked a watershed, praised by some, lamented by others, in Holiday's evolution from exuberant jazz singer to chanteuse of lovelorn pain and loneliness. Once Holiday added it to her repertoire, some of its sadness seemed to cling to her; as she deteriorated physically, the song took on new poignancy and immediacy. The jazz critic

Ralph J. Gleason even saw it as a metaphor for her entire life. "She really was happy only when she sang," he once wrote. "The rest of the time she was a sort of living lyric to the song 'Strange Fruit,' hanging, not on a poplar tree, but on the limbs of life itself."

In its own small way, "Strange Fruit" might even have accelerated Holiday's decline. Surely a song that forced a nation to confront its darkest impulses, a song that maligned an entire portion of the country, did not win her any friends in high places who might have cut her some slack as she degenerated into substance abuse and assorted scrapes with the law. "I've made lots of enemies, too," she told *Down Beat* in 1947, shortly after she was busted for drugs in Philadelphia. "Singing that ["Strange Fruit"] hasn't helped any. I was doing it at the Earle [Theater in Philadelphia] 'til they made me stop." William Dufty, the man who cowrote Holiday's autobiography, is convinced that Holiday shortchanged the creator of "Strange Fruit" because she felt the song only brought her grief—even leading her at one point to be hauled before red-baiting federal investigators.

After its initial run of popularity, "Strange Fruit" fell into disuse for many years—the victim of the conservatism of one era, the idealism and hopefulness of another, and the disillusionment of a third. Josh White and

Nina Simone were among the few artists to attempt it in the 1950s and 1960s. But recently many other musicians—from Sting to Dee Dee Bridgewater to Tori Amos to Cassandra Wilson to UB40 to Siouxsie and the Banshees—have recorded "Strange Fruit," each cut an act of courage given Holiday's continuing hold over the song. (That might not apply to 101 Strings, which recorded an orchestral version.) Sidney Bechet did an instrumental version shortly after Holiday's own record appeared; though it contained no words, Victor chose not to release it for many years.

The song now pops up in many places. Leon Litwack, the Pulitzer Prize–winning historian of the Civil War and Reconstruction periods, uses it in his classes at the University of California at Berkeley, and Stephen Bright cites it in "Capital Punishment: Race, Poverty and Disadvantage," a class he teaches in the law schools of Harvard, Yale, and Emory. Don Ricco, a teacher in Novato, California, plays it for his eighth-graders when they're studying the Civil War; while they review the tortured saga of American race relations, they can also learn about the power of metaphor. "Strange Fruit" is what Mickey Rourke inexplicably puts on his turntable to seduce Kim Basinger in 9 ½ Weeks (predictably, it fails miserably as mood music). A federal appeals court judge cited it a few years ago to show that execution by hanging was inherently "cruel and unusual." It was banned from South African radio during the apartheid era. Khallil Abdul Muhammad, Louis Farrakhan's notoriously anti-Semitic disciple and maestro of the "Million Man March," has quoted it in speeches assailing American racism—unaware, apparently, that the song was written by a white Jewish schoolteacher from New York City.

That schoolteacher, Abel Meeropol, who wrote under the pen name "Lewis Allan," had not written the song for Holiday; several others, including Meeropol's wife, Anne, had sung it before her. And yet, so completely did Holiday come to own "Strange Fruit" that Meeropol—who is better remembered nowadays for adopting the orphaned sons of Ethel and Julius Rosenberg following their parents' execution than for his thousands of other songs and poems—spent half a lifetime, starting with the moment the song became famous, reminding people that it was really his creation, and his alone.

It didn't always work; no one could seem to accept that so potent a song could come from so prosaic a source. Various articles saddled Meeropol with a wide range of purported collaborators. One French magazine described him as the headmaster of a school for blacks somewhere along the Mississippi. "One Lewis Allen [*sic*] is cited as the author of 'Strange Fruit,' but did he compose both words and music?" the composer and diarist Ned Rorem, a passionate Holiday devotee, wrote in the *New York Times* in 1995, nine years after Meeropol's death. "Indeed, who was he? Was he black?" (To the organizers of a celebration of music by black composers at the Virginia Museum of Fine Arts in 1999, the answer was yes, for they included "Strange Fruit" on the program.)

In a way, Meeropol sealed his particular fate, his status as a historical footnote, when he decided that it was Billie Holiday to whom he'd bring the song: she, more than any other artist ever could have, effectively made it her own. "Nobody could *say the words* even as Miss Holiday did," said Lena Horne, who as a child had fled a lynching in the small southern town in which her mother, an actress in a tent company, had been appearing. "It wasn't about singing. It was about feeling things artfully in your soul." "When you listen to her, it's almost like an audio tape of her autobiography," said Tony Bennett, who called "Strange Fruit" a "magnificent" song. "She didn't sing anything unless she had lived it."

I wrote "Strange Fruit" because I hate lynching and I hate injustice and I hate the people who perpetuate it.

—*Abel Meeropol, 1971*

I wrote
"Strange Fruit"

THE OPENING LINE OF Holiday's autobiography, *Lady Sings the Blues,* famously reads: "Mom and Pop were just a couple of kids when they got married. He was eighteen, she was sixteen, and I was three." Like so much in the book, this is not quite right; in fact, things were worse: Holiday's parents never married and were scarcely together at all, except at the carnival (or dance) in Baltimore on the night in the summer of 1914 when she was conceived.

Holiday was born in Philadelphia on April 7, 1915. That made her only twenty-four years old in 1939, but she had already experienced enough prejudice and despair by then—including time in a home for wayward black children, then in a whorehouse, where she first heard the recordings of Bessie Smith and Louis Armstrong—to call herself a "race woman." She began performing in Harlem in the late 1920s; by 1933, she had been discovered by the great record producer John Hammond, who quickly teamed her up with Benny Goodman, Teddy Wilson, and other legendary musicians of the day. Together, they made what became some of Holiday's finest and most beloved records: "I Wished on a Moon," "What a Little Moonlight Will Do," and "Me, Myself and I," to cite just three examples. In the late 1930s, she toured with the bands of Count Basie and Artie Shaw.

Though all of the hard knocks helped Holiday infuse a unique mixture of resilience, defiance, exuberance, and shrewdness into everything she sang, her songs, at least on paper, were invariably what her first biographer, Linda Kuehl, called "second cousins to her favorite reading: love comics and true romance magazines"—that is, bland, banal ballads. Politics, and particularly racial politics, had never influenced her choice of material until "Strange Fruit" came along.

Holiday's "autobiography"—cowritten by Dufty and entitled *Lady Sings the Blues* (the publisher insisted that "blues" be in the title, though Holiday herself had favored the last two words of "Strange Fruit": "bitter crop")—

offers an account of the song's origins that may set a new record for most misinformation per column inch. (Holiday later tried to fob off the blame on Dufty: "Shit, man, I ain't never read that book," she said. In fact, because her publisher was skittish about the entire undertaking, it made her read and sign every page of the manuscript. The embellishment was actually all Holiday's; she had been peddling much of the mythology for years. In fact, she told much of what appears in her autobiography to a Los Angeles newspaper columnist only three years after she introduced "Strange Fruit.") "The germ of the song was in a poem by Lewis Allen [*sic*]," Holiday declared in the book. "When he showed me that poem, I dug it right off. It seemed to spell out all the things that had killed Pop."

As Holiday told the story, her father, a musician in Fletcher Henderson's band, was exposed to poison gas as a soldier during World War I and died of pneumonia in 1937 after several segregated Southern hospitals refused to treat him. "Allen had heard how Pop died and of course was interested in my singing. He suggested that Sonny White, who had been my accompanist, and I turn it into music. So the three of us got together and did the job in about three weeks." (To the Los Angeles newspaperman, she had Meeropol coming into Café Society, and realizing upon hearing Holiday that were his anti-lynching poem set to music, she'd be "the one person in the whole entertainment world who could sing it.")

Meeropol told a very different story. An English teacher at De Witt Clinton High School in the Bronx for twenty-seven years, he had led two other, parallel lives. One was as a political activist: he and his wife were closet Communists, donating a percentage of their earnings to the Party (the FBI maintained that he had belonged only until 1947, though it continued to follow him for twenty-three years after that). The other was as a writer, poet, and composer. Meeropol had what Earl Robinson, the man who wrote "Ballad for Americans" and "Joe Hill," called "an inexhaustible ability to turn out topical lyrics." He wrote incessantly—poems, ballads, musicals, plays—all using the nom de plume "Lewis Allan," the names of his two natural-born children, neither of whom survived infancy. Many of his creations were political, albeit with a light touch: representative song titles include "Swing Away with Daladier," "The Chamberlain Crawl," and "Is There a Red Under Your Bed?" Though he had his admirers—Ira Gershwin, the German-American composer Kurt Weill ("his lyrics have great beauty and a quality of their own . . . I consider him a highly talented writer, a very conscientious worker, and a man of great integrity and high ideals"), and the Nobel Prize–winning novelist Thomas Mann wrote references for him when he applied for a Guggenheim Fellowship in the 1940s—most of his work was quickly forgotten and now sits in dusty heaps at Boston University. Apart from "Strange Fruit," he is best known for the lyrics to "The House I Live In" (a paean to tolerance cowritten by Earl Robinson and sung by Frank Sinatra in a short film that won a special Oscar in 1945), "Beloved Comrade" (written in 1936 for the Spanish Loyalists and often sung in tributes to Franklin Roosevelt, who is said to have liked it), and "Apples, Peaches, and Cherries" (once recorded by Peggy Lee).

Lynchings—during which blacks were murdered with unspeakable brutality, often in a carnival-like atmosphere, and then, with the acquiescence if not the complicity of local authorities, hung from trees for all to see—were rampant in the South following the Civil War and for many years thereafter. According to figures kept by the Tuskegee Institute—conservative figures—between 1889 and 1940, 3,833 people were lynched; ninety percent of them were murdered in the South, and four-fifths of them were black. Lynchings tended to occur in poor, small towns—often taking the place, the famed newspaper columnist H. L. Mencken once said, "of the merry-go-round, the theatre, the symphony orchestra." They involved either the whole community or a cabal of vigilantes, often in disguise. And they were meted out for a host of alleged offenses—not just for murder, theft, and rape, but for insulting a white person, boasting, swearing, or buying a car. In some instances, there was no infraction at all; it was just time to remind "uppity" blacks to stay in their place.

The numbers gradually declined; by the 1930s the days were long gone when the pioneering black civil rights leader W. E. B. Du Bois unfurled a banner declaring "Another Lynching Today" outside his New York office whenever one occurred. Officially, there were only three lynchings in 1939—the year Holiday first sang about them. (There were nonetheless signs that many more than that occurred but were hushed up, and that they were increasingly brutal and sadistic. "They used to be big mobs hunting for a nigger, but now you just hear about some nigger found hanging off a bridge," one observer reported.) Still, a survey taken in 1939 revealed that more than six in ten Southerners thought lynchings to be justified in cases of sexual assault. And despite a long campaign by the NAACP, Congress had never managed to pass a federal anti-lynching law.

Lynchings may have been localized affairs, but as Gunnar Myrdal pointed out in *An American Dilemma*, his classic 1944 study of race relations in the United States, they brutalized feelings everywhere. "Even in the North, some people have ceased to be concerned when another lynching occurs, and they jest about going South to see a lynching," he wrote. Meeropol, clearly, was not among them. In fact, it is possible that what inspired him to write "Strange Fruit" was a double lynching that took place north of the Mason-Dixon line—in Marion, Indiana, in 1930—immortalized in a shocking and widely publicized photograph. In any case, it was around that time that Meeropol, then in his early thirties, came across in a civil rights magazine a photograph of a particularly ghastly lynching, and he said it had haunted him for days. So he wrote a poem about it, one that the Communist journal *The New Masses* agreed in early 1936 to publish but that first saw print—as "Bitter Fruit"—in the January 1937 issue of *The New York Teacher*, a union publication.

Meeropol often asked others, most notably Earl Robinson, to set his poems to music. But with "Strange Fruit," he insisted on doing the task himself. The song was then performed regularly in left-wing circles—by Meeropol's wife, by progressive friends at gatherings in hotels and bungalow colonies around New York, by members of the local teachers union, by a black vocalist named Laura Duncan (including once at Madison Square Garden), and by a quartet of black singers at a fund-raiser for the anti-Fascists during the Spanish Civil War. As it happened, the co-producer of that fund-raiser, Robert Gordon, was also directing the first floor show at Café Society, which had opened in December 1938. The featured attraction: Billie Holiday, who had just quit Artie Shaw's band in part because she'd been forced to take the freight elevator during a gig at a New York hotel. And not just any hotel, but one named after Abraham Lincoln.

One of the first numbers we put on was called "Strange Fruit Grows on Southern Trees," the tragic story of lynching. Imagine putting that on in a nightclub!

—Nightclub owner Barney Josephson, 1942

tragic story of
lynching

CAFÉ SOCIETY—"a nightclub to take the stuffing out of stuffed shirts," where left-wing WPA types (Ad Reinhardt, John Groth, Adolph Dehn, Sidney Hoff, William Gropper) did the murals and a simian-looking Hitler hung from the ceiling by the coat check—was unusual even for New York City. Dubbing itself "the wrong place for the Right people," it mocked the empty celebrity worship, right-wing politics, snootiness, and racial discrimination of popular New York hangouts like the Stork Club.

At Café Society, the doormen wore rags and ragged white gloves and stood by as the customers opened the doors themselves; the bartenders were all veterans of the

Abraham Lincoln Brigade; blacks and whites fraternized on stage and off. As one press account described it, the club had "no girlie line, no smutty gags, no Uncle Tom comedy." George Avakian, the famed record producer, wrote that "the café was one of the 'good' places in which Negroes were permitted, and, if possible, given the best tables, while anyone in evening clothes would be placed behind a pillar or almost in the kitchen." Its politics were somewhere left of the New Deal; when Eleanor Roosevelt made what might have been her only foray into a New York nightclub, it was to Café Society that she went.

Located in a onetime basement speakeasy on Sheridan Square in Greenwich Village, christened by the columnist and playwright Clare Booth Luce (and commemorated today in the mosaic murals at the nearby subway stop), Café Society was the brainchild of Barney Josephson, a shoe salesman from Trenton, New Jersey, with progressive sympathies. Its patrons, the historian David Stowe has written, consisted of "labor leaders, intellectuals, writers, jazz lovers, celebrities, students and assorted leftists." As Michael Denning, an American Studies professor at Yale has put it, Café Society represented a unique synthesis of cultures, blending the politically radical cabarets of Weimar Berlin and Paris with the jazz clubs and revues of Harlem. In both its Village incarnation and at a second location in midtown Manhattan, Café Society attracted people like Nelson Rockefeller, Charlie Chaplin, Errol Flynn, Lauren Bacall, Lillian Hellman, Langston Hughes, and Paul Robeson; Lena Horne, Teddy Wilson, Sarah Vaughan, Imogene Coca, Carol Channing, and Zero Mostel performed there. It was probably the only place in America where "Strange Fruit" could have been sung and savored.

In January 1939, the *New York Sun* reported that Marc Blitzstein, author of the left-wing polemical opera "The Cradle Will Rock," had written a new song for Billie Holiday. Perhaps. But around the same time, according to Meeropol—who had never met Holiday and apparently knew nothing about her father, who probably never fought in Europe in World War I and is unlikely to have been gassed there—club owner Josephson and producer Gordon had asked him to bring "Strange Fruit" to the new nightclub. (According to Josephson, Meeropol just showed up there.) "I read the lyrics, and I was just floored by them," Josephson told British documentary filmmaker John Jeremy in 1983. "I said, 'What do you want to do with this?' He said, 'I would love to have Billie do this song.' " Shortly thereafter Meeropol sat down at Café Society's piano and played it for Holiday. Neither Tin Pan Alley nor jazz, closer to the cabaret tradition of Blitzstein than anything else, it was utterly alien to her, and she appeared indifferent. "I feel quite sure that if Barney Josephson and Bob Gordon had not been so impressed by the song, it may never have been sung by Billie Holiday because it was so different from the usual genre of songs to which she lent her unique voice and unforgetable [*sic*] musical interpretation," Meeropol later wrote. "To be perfectly frank, I didn't think she felt comfortable with the song. . . . I feel almost certain that if she had to choose from a number of songs at that time, it would not have been 'Strange Fruit.' " The Holiday he remembered was "not communicative at all" that day and had asked only one question about the song: what did "pastoral" mean?

Josephson, who rarely asked Holiday to perform anything, later maintained that she "didn't know what the hell the song meant" and sang it originally only as a favor to him. "She looked at me after [Meeropol had] finished and said, 'What do you want me to do with that, man?' and I said, 'It would be wonderful if you'd sing it. If you care to. You don't have to.' And she said, 'You wants me to sing it? I sings it.' And she sang it." Not until a few months later, when he spotted a tear running down her cheek during one performance, was Josephson convinced that she had finally grasped just what those strange fruit were. "I gotta tell you the truth," he liked to tell people years after. "She sang it just as well when she didn't know what it was about."

Holiday, it is true, was in some ways unsophisticated, famous for reading nothing more serious than comic books, and the song was unlike anything she had done: social commentary rather than some first-person ditty about love and romance. Josephson's version of events nonetheless seems harsh and patronizing. That Holiday could not have known precisely what she was singing about and felt it deeply is quite inconceivable. Still, the question of precisely what she understood the song to mean arose repeatedly in her life.

In her autobiography, Holiday claimed that she was eager to perform the new song. "Some guy's brought me a hell of a damn song that I'm going to do," she said she told the leader of her backup band, Frankie Newton. One way or another, Holiday took "Strange Fruit" and began experimenting with it. She may have had her first audience for it at a party in Harlem in late 1938, to which, one eyewitness recalled, she arrived in the wee hours clutching the sheet music like a schoolgirl carrying her books. The reaction of the party-goers would prove typical. "I would like to sing a new song which I have been rehearsing all day; it's called 'Strange Fruit.' I want to see what you all think of it," she told her listeners, a young salesman named Charles Gilmore among them. Up to that moment, Gilmore recalled, the party had been a raucous affair. But as Holiday sang and the lyrics sank in, the crowd grew still; the apartment became a cathedral, the party a funeral. "That was all she sang; nobody asked her to sing anything else," he said. "There was a finality about the last note. Even the pianist knew. He just got up and walked away. It was an odd thing. Nobody clapped or anything." But after an interval of silence there were yells of encouragement: "You did it again, girl!" "Great song!" Some urged her to perform it before a larger audience. And she soon did.

According to Meeropol, who went to Café Society to hear her introduce the song, Holiday sang "Strange Fruit" with conviction and understanding from the beginning. "She gave a startling, most dramatic and effective interpretation, which could jolt an audience out of its complacency anywheres [*sic*]," he wrote. "This was exactly what I wanted the song to do and why I wrote it. Billie Holiday's styling of the song was incomparable and fulfilled the bitterness and shocking quality I had hoped the song would have. The audience gave her a tremendous ovation."

So did Holiday grasp the meaning of "Strange Fruit" or was she oblivious to it all? Barry Ulanov, a jazz scholar who heard her sing it while he was a student at Columbia, suggested a third alternative: Holiday understood the song but was uncomfortable with it and was particularly uncomfortable that others were pressuring her to sing something that made her uncomfortable. That she sang it with such ferocity and anger, he speculated, reflected both what the song said and what she wanted to say herself: *So you say you want to hear about lynching, do you? Well then I'm really going to give it to you!* "She was not out there simply making a social or political plea," Ulanov said. "She was saying something in her own complex way."

One story—by way of Madeline Gilford, the widow of Jack Gilford, the comedian who was Café Society's emcee—has it that Holiday's mother objected when she began singing "Strange Fruit" and asked her why she was doing it. Because it could make things better, Holiday replied.

"But you'll be dead," her mother insisted.

"Yeah, but I'll feel it," Holiday said. "I'll know it in my grave."

Whatever her initial unease, Holiday quickly laid claim to the song, telling audiences it had been written especially for her, and resenting anyone else—like Josh White—who dared to sing it. "The audience [at Café Society, where White appeared for several years in the 1940s] shouted for [White] to leave the song alone," she boasted in her autobiography. White, who began singing "Strange Fruit" in 1944 with the torch singer and actress Libby Holman, later wrote that Holiday initially wanted "to cut my throat" for performing it. At least according to one story, that was literally true: It is said that one night Holiday charged into White's dressing room at Café Society with a knife and held it to his Adam's apple. "Billie, we should be singing this song until we never have to sing it again," he told her. "We shouldn't be fighting about it." She evidently agreed; there was no homicide that night, and both kept including it in their programs. "We got to be friendly. Well, after we got over the 'Strange Fruit' thing, we became friendly," White wrote in a tribute to Holiday shortly after her death. "I didn't want to steal anything from Billie. I loved her interpretation of the song, but I wanted to do 'Strange Fruit' my way."

No one ever tampered with Meeropol's words. But Arthur Herzog, who wrote two other legendary songs often misattributed solely to Holiday ("Don't Explain" and "God Bless the Child"), claimed that it was an arranger, Danny Mendelsohn, who was really responsible for the song's ultimate sound. "He [Meeropol] wrote something or other alleged to be music and Barney [Josephson] gave it to Danny and Danny rewrote it. Put it into shape," Herzog later said. "Whether he rewrote it or discarded it, I don't know." (Herzog later said that when "Strange Fruit" was recorded, another of his compositions was to have been on the flip side. But, thankfully, he hadn't gone to the studio that day: Anything called "Swing, Black Man, Swing" would have poorly complemented an anti-lynching song.) In fact, Holiday bent and twisted and tweaked every song she ever sang and surely played with "Strange Fruit" too. Martin Brin, who had performed the song among Meeropol's left-wing friends in the Catskills long before Holiday had ever heard of it, said he went about the task very differently. "I was a little disappointed [with Holiday's version] because it sounded a little like jazz," he recalled. "We sang it with sort of a zip, with punch."

Witnessing "Strange Fruit" at Café Society was a visual, as well as an auditory, experience. Josephson, who called the song "agitprop" (that is, agitation and propaganda for left-wing causes), decreed elaborate stage directions for each of the three nightly performances. Holiday was to close each set with it. Before she began, all service stopped. Waiters, cashiers, busboys were all immobilized. The room went completely dark, save for a pin spot on Holiday's face. When she was finished and the lights went out, she was to walk off the stage, and no matter how thunderous the ovation, she was never to return for a bow. "My instruction was to walk off, period," Josephson later said. "People had to remember 'Strange Fruit,' get their insides burned with it." Miscreants were apparently dealt with harshly. "At Café Society I used to wonder at how quiet for a nightclub it was when I sang," Holiday recalled in 1949. "I found out later the waiters made a habit of going up to the noisiest characters and saying 'Miss Holiday is afraid you aren't enjoying yourself. Pay up and go.' "

Of course, Holiday was quite capable of registering her unhappiness herself. Barney Josephson recalled the time when the singer, displeased with an audience she considered square or noisy or inattentive, let them have it after a couple of songs. "She turned her back, bowed, picked up her gown and showed her black ass," he said. "They gasped. There was a hush. I gave Teddy Wilson the cue and the orchestra went into a dance. I told Billie never to do that again. She said 'Fuck 'em,' but she never did it. That was one time a black person said 'kiss my ass' to a white audience and showed it."

But while Josephson wanted the audience to feel "burned," the flames were quickly doused, according to Heywood Hale Broun, then a student at Swarthmore College and later a longtime reporter at CBS News. In 1939 Broun wrote in his father's magazine, *Broun's Nutmeg*, that Holiday's rendition of "Strange Fruit" was "one of the most gripping things" he had ever heard. ("It is hard to describe this expressive emotional quality but there is a word for it and that word is blues," he added.) But years later, he recalled that after a short interval, Josephson quickly had the musicians go into something light, just to cut the tension. "After we'd oohed and aahed in our kind of liberal way, the band would hit a sharp chord and then go into 'Them There Eyes,' " he recalled. "This always broke the mood. I thought this was weak of him—to come back to 'Hey, we're really just a nightclub and this is one of those happy black songs.' " Broun's Swarthmore classmate, Alden Todd, sensed a similar incongruity: "The contrast between a tragic song of protest sung with deep feelings by a Negro woman who felt the horror of a lynching, and the patrons out for a good time drinking and at times yakking, some of them oblivious to the message of the singer.

"I wondered then whether it made sense to sing such a song in such a milieu," he continued. "I thought it belonged instead in a concert setting, without beer and whiskey and cigarette smoke."

And there she came out [of Café Society] and she was scream-ing, "Renie, I tried to kill him, I tried to kill him, I tried to . . ." And I said, "What is wrong, Lady?" And she told me then that there was this fella—a white man from Georgia, you know, one of those Georgia crackers—who was sitting ringside and drinking and Lady was doing "Strange Fruit." And when Lady was on her way out of the club, he yelled, "Come here, Billie." She went thinking he wanted to buy her a drink, but he said "I want to show you some 'strange fruit,' " and . . . well, he made this very obscene picture on his napkin and the way he had it, honey, it was awful! And she picked up the chair and hit him on the head, and before it was over, she showed him, honey, because she went crazy. I mean that she was sweeping up the floor with this man, honey, and they said—the owner and bouncer at Café Society—said, "Go on, Lady. We'll take care of him," and they threw him out right on his ears.

—*Songwriter Irene Wilson, 1971*

Café Society

To some, Andy Razaf's "Black and Blue," written in 1929 and immortalized by Louis Armstrong, was arguably the first black protest song aimed at a largely white audience. But while lynching was a conspicuous theme in black fiction, theater, and art, it did not feature prominently in black music. Irving Berlin referred to lynching in "Supper Time" (a song Ethel Waters made famous), but before Meeropol and Holiday came along, no one had ever confronted the topic so directly. "It was really the first time that anyone had so explicitly and poetically transmitted the message of black people," said the noted record producer Ahmet Ertegun. "It was always guarded in the blues: hidden language. But this was quite open."

To the hip young liberals who came to hear Holiday amid what the columnist Ralph de Toledano later called "the eddying cigarette smoke" of Café Society, or to the college kids who paid seventy-five cents to stand and listen at the bar, "Strange Fruit" left an indelible impression. "It had its power and validity in the exquisite torture of her voice and in the ungainly beauty of a dark face starkly delineated by the baby spots," Toledano later wrote. It was "a beautifully rendered thing, like a great, dramatic moment in the theater," the artist and cartoonist Al Hirschfeld said. "To see Billie Holiday alone was something else, but this particular song made one sit and listen and think." To the songwriters Adolph Green and Betty Comden, who sauntered over to Café Society with pals like Judy Holliday, the actress, and Leonard Bernstein after their nightly gig at the nearby Village Vanguard, watching Billie Holiday was unforgettable. "It was thrilling," Comden recalled. "That song was bloodcurdling and wonderful and she did it so beautifully." "She was shocking in her personal magnetism," Ralph Gleason, the jazz writer, later recalled. "Standing there with a thin spotlight on her great, sad face, and a gardenia in her hair, she sang 'Strange Fruit' and 'Fine and Mellow' and the singers were never the same thereafter."

To younger black performers like Lena Horne, the

song's impact was both more instinctive and more imme-diate. As a child Horne had toured the South with her mother, an actress in a tent company. Once, the troupe had to flee the small Florida town in which it was appear-ing when a lynching occurred there. "So when I was a lit-tle girl I knew about the fear it aroused in my people and in my mother," she recalled seventy-five years later. "It's something that I wanted to forget, but it stayed with me, before and after." Holiday, Horne said, "was putting into words what so many people had seen and lived through. She seemed to be performing in melody and words the same thing I was feeling in my heart." Horne, who later had her own long run at Café Society, saw Holiday per-form it only once. "She was angry," Horne remembered. "Many people had realized that tears weren't doing any good." Never, though, did it occur to Horne to per-form the song herself; "Strange Fruit" belonged to Billie Holiday.

Vernon Jarrett Remembers

True, lynchings had largely disappeared from the Ameri-can landscape when "Strange Fruit" was first sung. But they remained oddly immediate, too. As Vernon Jarrett, who grew up in Tennessee and later became a newspa-

perman in Chicago, put it, black children and teenagers in the 1930s invariably knew older people who'd witnessed a lynching and told the kinds of stories about it that kept young people up nights. There were stories of white people fighting among themselves for the dead man's fingers or toes, or pickling his penis and keeping it in a jar in the local barbershop. Or stories of white people putting on their Sunday best to attend lynchings, or even their uniforms from World War I or the Spanish-American War, as if racism was real patriotism: "I am a real American. I lynch black folks. I keep them in their places." To Jarrett this was, in a more refined form, what the Congress of the United States had declared by refusing over and over again to pass an anti-lynching bill. Then there were people like Jarrett's parents, who, while never actually lynched themselves, had been humbled in a hundred other ways that amounted to nearly the same thing. And, growing up in the South, there was always the feeling among blacks that were they ever to step out of line, to look the wrong way at a white woman or be perceived to have done so, they could wind up at the wrong end of a rope. All of this came to Jarrett's mind when he heard Holiday sing "Strange Fruit" in New York during the summer of 1947.

"It was indescribable, man," he said. "She was stand-
ing up there singing this song as though this was for real,
as if she had just witnessed a lynching. That's what
knocked me out. I thought she was about to cry. She was
looking at no one in the audience. She could have been a
little high, like she was singing to herself: 'This is for me.
Fuck all of you.' She impressed me as someone who had
also been wronged, as if she'd been lynched herself in
some fashion or another. There was a sense of resigna-
tion, as if 'these people are going to have power for a long
time and I can't do a damn thing about it except put it
in a song.' When I heard her sing I heard other kinds of
lynchings, not just hanging from trees. I saw my own
mother and father, two college-educated people, and all
the crap they had to go through. Only three white men
ever called my father 'Mister,' and one of them later
acted as though it was a mistake. To me, that was part of
the whole lynch syndrome, the lynching of the body and
the spirit put together. That's the way her face looked
when she sang that. All over this woman was the fact
that 'we're all taking a screwing, someone is messing
with us, this is a fucked-up situation'—like she was
psychoanalyzing herself and the black condition, telling
us there were 'no escape' signs up, regardless of how great

you were. I don't think it was just that she was high. She
was making her peace with her own lynched existence.
This is how most of us felt. . . . It enhanced my commit-
ment to changing this stuff, that's what it did. I once
heard 'Strange Fruit' while I was driving and I tried to
park the car, out of respect for her—just to let her voice
sink in."

✍

Critical reactions to Holiday's performance of "Strange Fruit" were mixed. *Harper's Bazaar* heralded Holiday as "a high priestess of swing" and touted "a new song in her repertoire that has to do with lynching, 'Strange Fruit Grows on Tropical Trees.' " (Inexplicably, no one ever seemed to get the name of the song right.) The English jazz writer Leonard Feather, whose association with Holiday was to last the rest of her life, wrote in the British magazine *Melody Maker* in April 1939 that at Café Society, Holiday "stood in a small jet of light, turned on her most wistful expression for the mike, and sang a number written specially for her, 'Strange Fruit,' a grim and moving piece about lynching down South." ("With John Hammond in charge of entertainments and a group of young left-wingers behind the scenes, it is no wonder that the music is swell here, and that the usual ruling against the acceptance of colored people as customers does not prevail," he also noted.) "The 'Fruit' number," *Variety* said, "has an undefined appeal though it's basically a depressing piece. There's no compromise with Miss Holiday's stuff: either patrons like her very much or they don't care for her at all."

But people began requesting "Strange Fruit" and it quickly became part of Holiday's routine, even though she said it made her sick to perform it. "I have to sing it," she once said. " 'Fruit' goes a long way in telling how they mistreat Negroes down South." Soon, Café Society began advertising not just Holiday—referred to in press accounts as "the buxom, colored songstress" or "the sepian songstress"—but the song itself. "HAVE YOU HEARD? 'Strange Fruit growing on Southern trees' sung by Billie Holiday" an advertisement in *The New Yorker* asked in March 1939.

Obviously, the song was destined to be "waxed," to use the contemporary term. But getting "Strange Fruit" on disc would not be easy. The man who'd discovered Billie Holiday and produced her records, John Hammond, didn't much like the song, and Columbia—apparently fearful of antagonizing Southern customers—wanted no part of it. So Holiday convinced Milt Gabler of Commodore Records, a small left-wing company defined by its progressive repertoire of artists and run out of a music store on East 42nd Street, to do it instead.

On April 20, 1939, in a studio at Fifth Avenue and 55th Street, Holiday and the musicians—Sonny White (to whom Holiday was once briefly engaged) on the piano, Frankie Newton on trumpet, Tab Smith on alto sax, Kenneth Hollon and Stan Payne on tenor sax, Jimmy McLin on guitar, John Williams on bass, Eddie Dougherty on drums—made what was to become the first and most famous recording of "Strange Fruit." It took four hours to complete because, Hollon later said, Gabler "wanted to get a great one out there." Also recorded that day were "Fine and Mellow" (which went on the flip side and developed a great following of its own), "Yesterdays," and "I Got a Right to Sing the Blues." At a dollar apiece, Commodore's 10-inch records were considerably more expensive than most. Concerned that customers would feel cheated by too short a cut, Gabler had White improvise his now-familiar, haunting overture; given the song's climactic close, one could hardly tack on anything at the end. The record was released in mid-1939.

Gabler gave Holiday five hundred dollars for the four sides, plus a thousand dollars later. How much she eventually earned for the songs he could not say. "We used to give her cash, especially when she was in trouble, right out of the cash register in the store," he said. "We never really kept a record of it."

Now in his eighties, Gabler lives in New Rochelle, New York. Not long ago, he fetched an antique LP from his archive for a visitor, then laid it down with shaky hands on an ancient turntable. Amid its scratches and static came the sound of White on the piano, playing "in a manner that is almost too gracious for the occasion," as the musical scholar Gunther Schuller has observed. (And, Schuller noted, White is playing in B-flat minor—a key Chopin and other composers have used for their more somber pieces.) Then came the utterly distinctive sound of Holiday herself. She is grim and purposeful, yet still with a lovely lightness to her. The overt editorializing is minimal; there is no weepiness, nor histrionics. Her elocution is superb, with but a hint of a Southern accent; her tone is languorous but unflinching, raw yet smooth, youthful yet worldly. The prevailing sentiment is not grief or defeat but contempt and confidence, detectable as she spits out the references to Southern gallantry and the sweetly scented magnolias. ("When Billie Holiday sings the phrase 'pastoral scene of the gallant South,' civilization has said its last word about the realpolitik of racial discrimination in all its forms and degrees," the British jazz critic Benny Green has written. "The resigned bitterness and contempt with which Billie throws out the phrase leaves nothing to be said.") But the intensity mounts until she reaches the word "crop," which dangles for a time back and forth on a strangely unresolved note like the dead man on the branch.

People still marvel at the performance and how understated and elegant it is. The Anglo-Irish jazz writer and composer Spike Hughes once lamented over how Bessie Smith had never sung "Strange Fruit," because "it is a song that needs to burn with the fierce fire of anger, as well as the flames of pathos." In fact, Holiday's subtlety makes it all the more powerful. "It is Billie's pure, un-self-pitying, distilled-emotion approach to the material that haunts our memories," Schuller writes. "The lyrics, which could have become obvious and maudlin, are treated with cold respect for the awesome facts. The hurt is there, but it is not worn on the sleeve. It never slobbers, Billie's poignant, finely textured voice threading a wary course between the potential pitfalls of pretentious social drama and awkwardly 'serious' pop balladry."

Ned Rorem, the composer and diarist, makes largely the same point. "Like most great pop singers—Piaf, Lenya—the less they do, the better," he said. "You don't need to prove the point because words and music are proving the point, and Billie seemed to have known that instinctively. All she did was simply close her eyes and throw her head back. She just sings it. She doesn't make grand opera out of it, the way Barbra Streisand would." Or, as Artie Shaw, the former bandleader, put it: "Nothing in her history can explain it. She never had any dramatic experience, but there was a sense of inherent drama in her. I don't think she ever took any elocution lessons, but when she said 'bitter' she said it in a way worthy of any Dame on the British stage. She always had that quality."

Warren Morse Remembers

When it first came out, "Strange Fruit" created its own set of evangelists, carrying around their copies of the Commodore 78. One was a labor organizer from New York named Warren Morse. He played it for some friends, breaking them in by first playing "Fine and Mellow" ("The woman I was with was just shocked by that. To her it was just sex, sex, sex, fuck, fuck, fuck"), then "Strange Fruit" ("She just sat there, stunned"). He took the record to places where people had never heard of Billie Holiday, let alone "Strange Fruit": first to Wisconsin, then to Missouri, where he played it once for some

white undergraduates at the state university. "They had
never heard anything remotely like this," he said.
"They'd never even heard anyone speaking about lynch-
ing. I remember one girl just broke down and started
sobbing. I was propagandizing, spreading the word. It
made an impact on people. For the first time in their
lives it made them think about the lynching victims as
humans, as people."

✍

The musicians had high expectations for the song. "The
words were so true; that's why the fellows thought it was
going to be a hit. But we didn't think it was going to be as
big as it was," said John Williams, the bassist that day. One
of the saxophonists, Kenneth Hollon, later said the record
sold 10,000 copies in its first week. (That seems exagger-
ated; according to *The New Yorker*, by 1945 it had sold
50,000 copies.) Meeropol, who had failed to copyright
"Strange Fruit" because he thought it had no commercial
possibilities, learned it had been recorded only when a
friend brought him the Commodore 78. After threatening
to hire a lawyer, he ultimately got standard royalties: two
cents per record, one for the words, another for the
music. He also got a small measure of celebrity, at least in

left-wing circles. "We all celebrated the fact that he wrote 'Strange Fruit,' " said Carl Reiner, then a young comic who worked with Meeropol at a bungalow colony in upstate New York in the summer of 1942.

Sheet music sales, however, were disappointing. "Your song is being sung around more than ever but only, unfortunately, at gatherings which are progressive," his publisher, Herbert Marks, wrote Meeropol in May 1940. (Laura Duncan had been applauded for it at the National Negro Congress, he noted, but ovations didn't equal revenues.) In May 1941, Marks dutifully reported to Meeropol that he was thus far entitled to all of two dollars in royalties for the year. "People say flattering things about [the song]," Marks lamented, "but they just don't go out and buy it."

Nonetheless, some people were acutely interested in how much Meeropol had earned from the song, and where those earnings were going. Forced to testify in 1941 before a state probe of Communist "subversion" in New York's public schools (he'd originally driven to Mexico to duck the subpoena), Meeropol was asked whether the Communist Party had paid him for "Strange Fruit" or if he'd donated whatever he'd earned from it to the Party. "I have never done any work for the Communist Party, I have never been paid by the Communist Party, I have nothing to do with the Communist Party," he replied. In any case, the pennies mounted: according to Bob Golden of Carlin America, longtime publishers of "Strange Fruit," the Meeropols, father and sons, have collected more than $300,000 from the song over the past sixty years.

This is about a phonograph record which has obsessed me for two days. It is called "Strange Fruit," and it will, even after the tenth hearing, make you blink and hold onto your chair. Even now, as I think of it, the short hair on the back of my neck tightens and I want to hit somebody. And I think I know who.

—*Columnist Samuel Grafton,*
New York Post, *October 1939*

"Strange Fruit"

ACCORDING TO one compilation, "Strange Fruit" the record made it to number sixteen on the charts in July 1939. Such lists from that era are notoriously unreliable, but the song was widely publicized, particularly in the left-wing press. *The New Masses* called it "the first successful attempt of white men to write blues." It continued: "The song is a superb outcry against lynching, remarkable because the lyrics are not too pretentious for the simple blues language."

More surprisingly, the song also made waves in the mainstream press. In a piece entitled "Strange Record," *Time* described the ballad as "a prime piece of musical propaganda for the NAACP" and printed the first verse of

"Allan's grim and gripping lyrics." ("Billie Holiday is a roly poly young colored woman with a hump in her voice," the article began. "She does not care enough about her figure to watch her diet, but she loves to sing." See photo insert.) Barney Josephson later insisted that the photograph of Holiday that accompanied the article was the first ever of a black person in the pages of *Time* or *Life*. In May 1939 *Variety* also heralded the song's imminent appearance. "Anti-Lynch Propaganda in Swingtime, on a Disc," it declared.

Surely the most extravagant praise came from Samuel Grafton, a columnist for the *New York Post*, then the most liberal of the city's many daily newspapers. "It hits, hard," he wrote. "It is as if a game of let's pretend had ended and a blues singer who had been hiding her true sorrow in a set of love ditties had lifted the curtain and told us what it was that made her cry." To Grafton, the song was "a fantastically perfect work of art, one which reversed the usual relationship between a black entertainer and her white audience: 'I have been entertaining you,' she seems to say, 'now you just listen to me.' The polite conventions between race and race are gone. It is as if we heard what was spoken in the cabins, after the night riders had clattered by." Grafton's concluding language was apocalyptic. "If the anger of the exploited ever mounts high enough in the South," he thundered, "it now has its Marseillaise."

The record made its way abroad. An editor of the *Times* of London, on assignment in the United States while German submarines were sinking British ships prior to World War II, stopped by the Commodore shop shortly before returning home, and bought two copies of "Strange Fruit"—one to take with him, the other to be shipped. That way, he told Milt Gabler, "one of us will get through."

Around the country, teenagers played "Strange Fruit" for one another with a sense of furtiveness, as if the fruit involved wasn't so much strange as forbidden. In Chicago, a buddy played the record for fifteen-year-old Ned Rorem and his friends, taking care to put "Fine and Mellow" on first so that everyone could grow accustomed to Holiday's distinctive voice. One of his mates was unimpressed with "Strange Fruit." "Frankenstein's theme song," she called it. But for Rorem, the session was an epic event: "My world changed forever," he was to write. "The graphic couplets about a lynching, grotesque and hopeless, rhythmless and dangerously slow, declaimed in a vulnerable velvet whine, were like nothing heard before." He went to hear Holiday when she appeared in Chicago's Panther Room a few months later, even though he was still underage.

Proponents of federal anti-lynching legislation urged that copies of the song be sent to Congress, where Southern senators were about to filibuster another bill to death.

"Let them constantly feel the terror of lynching, the threat to democracy which is inherent in the flouting of democratic processes," a magazine called *The Fraternal Outlook* urged its readers in March 1939. "The [New York] Theatre Arts Committee last week made a unique plea to the individual members of the U.S. Senate by sending them a copy of Lewis Allen's [*sic*] song, 'Strange Fruit,' one of the strongest indictments of lynching ever penned," another publication reported. "Literally millions of Americans, the senators were told, have found the words of 'Strange Fruit' terribly and strangely moving." Within a few years, Lillian Smith took the name for the title of her famous antisegregation novel. Holiday's claim that Smith, a Southerner herself, told her the song had inspired her to write the book is fanciful. But Smith acknowledged Meeropol on the title page and came to Café Society once to hear Holiday sing. (After the show she went backstage; Holiday seemed stoned to her.)

Within a few months of its debut on disc, "Strange Fruit" had become an integral part of Holiday's repertoire. By October 1939 the *New York Sun* was describing the singer and the song as "practically inseparable." Still, many jazz purists never liked "Strange Fruit" or what they thought it did to Billie Holiday. "Perhaps I expected too much of 'Strange Fruit,' the ballyhooed . . . tune which, via gory wordage and hardly any melody, expounds an anti-lynching campaign," a *Down Beat* critic wrote. "At least I'm sure it's not for Billie."

More famously, John Hammond called the song "artistically the worst thing that ever happened" to Holiday. "The beginning of the end for Billie was 'Strange Fruit,' when she had become the darling of the left-wing intellectuals," he said. "I think she began taking herself seriously, and thinking of herself as very important. . . . As soon as pop artists think they are contributing to art, something happens to their art. . . . She became mannered, and that's the thing I disliked most in any pop artist. This kind of thing never happened to Bessie Smith. She never had that kind of success with white people, for one thing—one of the luckiest things that ever happened to her. But Billie had it. And homosexuals just *fell* for Billie."

Holiday sensed, and resented, Hammond's condescension. Indeed, his disapproval may have prompted her to perform the song. "Aw, John's square, John's just rich, John wants to run my life, tries to tell me and everybody else what to do," she once said. (Hammond was also responsible for spreading some misinformation about the song, for example, that Holiday had originally learned it from Josh White.)

Norman Granz, who included Holiday in his famous "Jazz at the Philharmonic" series in the 1940s and recorded her last great work on Mercury and Verve Records after that, called Hammond's assessment "a load of crap." "I don't really think one could say that under any circumstances Billie took herself seriously," he said. "To the contrary, Billie was down to earth. For John to say that the song destroyed her ... what the hell was she doing plunging that thing into her arm all the time? That's what screwed Billie up, that and the men that beat her up all the time."

But Hammond, who died in 1987, was not alone in his beliefs. "Moving propaganda, perhaps, but not poetry and not art," is how the late jazz scholar Martin Williams described "Strange Fruit." "Very few of us really liked that song," said Jerry Wexler, the veteran record producer. "It's so un–Billie Holiday. It's got too much of an agenda. A lot of people who had tin ears and who wouldn't know a melody if it hit them in the head embraced the song only because of the politics. It's so polemical, and musically it has very little to recommend it in terms of a melodic line, and the melodic line was her meat. I absolutely approve of the sentiment. I think it's a great lyric. But it doesn't interest me as a song."

Evelyn Cunningham, who worked in the New York office of the *Pittsburgh Courier*, one of the nation's leading black newspapers in the 1940s, doubted the sincerity of both Billie Holiday and her listeners. "The song did not disturb me because I never had the feeling that this was something she was very, very serious about," she said. "It was a unique kind of song, an attention grabber, and for me it was out of kilter completely with what she had done and what she was doing. I always thought 'Strange Fruit' was a marketing device for her. It created a lot of attention. I don't think she really understood or anticipated the serious attention that came about. . . . Many times in nightclubs when I heard her sing the song it was not a sadness I sensed as much as there was something else; it's got to do with sexuality. Men and women would hold hands, they would look at each other, and they would pretend there was love going on, or something sexual. They would get closer together and yet there was a veneer—and just a veneer—of anger and concern. . . . There comes a time in a black person's life where you're up to your damned ears in lynching and discrimination, when sometimes you were just so sick of it, but it was heresy to express it. She was a great artist and she did great things with that song, but you would not admit that you did not want to hear it."

Some jazz aficionados saw things differently. For instance, "Strange Fruit" was one of the six Holiday recordings deemed most notable by the editors of the *Jazz Record Book* in 1942. "Billie's sympathetic and faithful interpretation of the realistic lyrics of 'Strange Fruit' makes this one of the most effective of the 'socially conscious' songs," they reported. Far from viewing it as a departure, critic Benny Green considered "Strange Fruit" integrally entwined with the rest of Holiday's work. Its power, he wrote, "could only have been gained by an artist steeped in the very quintessence of the jazz art all her life. The rise and fall of the phrases, the shaping of the words, the feeling for a dying cadence and the occasional slight amendment or variation of the melody, these are the exclusive weapons of the jazz artist. No other musician can possibly have access to them."

The late folksinger Laura Nyro, whose mother introduced her to "Strange Fruit," spotted the same thread. "I read a couple of things in an album jacket that said when she started getting into singing 'Strange Fruit' that's when the music ended," Nyro said of Holiday, whom she called "the great mother-musician-teacher of the art of phrasing." "And I feel the opposite: that was her art and her consciousness just traveling deeper." That was apparently how Holiday herself saw things.

"Billie came to see me at Café Society Uptown [around

1941] and she told me that she really found herself with the singing whereas everyone felt she had found herself before," the pianist Teddy Wilson, who played with Holiday throughout the 1930s, remembered many years later. "But she was singing very much to her own personal satisfaction. She was just beginning to hear herself."

Holiday left Café Society after nine months, moving up to the jazz clubs of West 52nd Street: Kelly's Stable, The Onyx, The Famous Door, and The Three Deuces, among others. The atmosphere there was less progressive—as a black woman, Holiday sometimes couldn't mix with the clientele—and more druggy (a cop asked one club owner to keep the marijuana smoking inside because his horses were getting stoned). But here, too, "Strange Fruit" went over well. One habitué of the street recalled her first encounter with the song. "The audience was really in a hush," she said. "It was the first time I remember being in a place that was so quiet. She had a captive audience."

When it came to singing "Strange Fruit," Holiday chose her spots carefully. In New York, apart from 52nd Street, she confined herself to places like Harlem and Union Square, where she sang it on May Day 1941. "No one, by the way, has been able to put over this as well as Billie," New York's *Amsterdam News* reported on that occasion. Out of town, she favored black theaters and concert halls and progressive nightclubs, most of them owned by Jews. In 1942, for instance, she sang it at Billy Berg's Trouville Club in Los Angeles, where a columnist for the *Los Angeles Daily News*, Ted Le Berthon, caught up with her afterwards. The song, he subsequently wrote in an open "letter" to Holiday, was something "no expert record collector is without." The mainstream record companies "sure kicked themselves," he continued, because the disc "has proved one of the greatest of all sellers."

"You went on to say how the bitter sorrow of your father's unnecessary death crept into your singing of 'Strange Fruit,' " the letter went on. "You have a tremendous white following, and many white friends in the show business for whom you have a deep affection and didn't want to be bitter, but you loved your father. Anyhow, bitterness is not part of your nature. So you put all the bitterness in you into that one song, and that's what helps give it that terrible reality."

Sometimes, she sang it in private homes. Harry Levin, a journalist then helping to run the Office of War Information in New York, recalled how one Saturday evening during the early days of World War II, after her work was done, Holiday unwound in the Greenwich Village apartment of the songwriter Arthur Herzog. Once Herzog began playing his most famous composition, "God Bless the Child," Holiday obligingly started singing it. "But we were not prepared for what followed," Levin recalled more than fifty years later. "Her face had changed utterly. Her body seemed to spring away from the piano. Her eyes were closed tightly. We were virtually paralyzed as she pulled us into physical contact with every word and gesture of 'Strange Fruit.' We sat stunned, silent, not daring to look at one another. In the midst of World War II, we were fighting to restore freedom. Was Billie reminding us that there was unfinished business which America should not overlook? In a long life, it remains my most cherished musical memory."

Holmes "Daddy-O" Daylie Remembers

In the early 1940s, before beginning a long and distinguished career as a disc jockey in Chicago, "Daddy-O" Daylie tended bar in the basement of the old Du Sable Hotel on the city's South Side, where black musicians like Holiday hung out while in town. Sometimes, after a drink or two, Holiday would go upstairs to Daylie's room, where she would listen to records, including some of her own. "Strange Fruit" was always among them, and always the last one she'd play. The Victrola would then reset itself, and play it again, and again and again.

When she was blue, it seemed to comfort her; when she was up, it buoyed her. Once, she made off with Daylie's old, brittle 10-inch disc of "Strange Fruit"—she never could manage to keep her own copy—and Daylie just looked the other way. "I knew she took my record and I let her keep it, because she wanted it so bad," he said.

"She would sit there and listen to it and she would cry," he recalled. "That's the one she wanted to hear. It didn't make any difference whether the song before was 'Me, Myself and I' or something else with [the famed saxophonist] Lester Young; when 'Strange Fruit' would come on, her face would change, she would become very pensive, and it would be like a funeral in the room. There might be eight of us in there, and not a word would be spoken. I would always try to get into her thoughts, but I didn't want to press too hard. And that was the end, that was like a finale. After 'Strange Fruit' anything else would be anticlimactic. We'd know the party was over; there was no need to put anything else on."

∾

In September 1942, Holiday happened to be appearing in Chicago when Studs Terkel was going off to the army, and she offered to come by and sing something at his farewell party. "She said, 'What would you like to hear, Baby?' and I said, 'Well, it's a toss-up: 'Fine and Mellow' of course, and 'Strange Fruit,' " Terkel remembered. "She sang both." Fifteen years later, near the end of Holiday's life, he heard her sing it twice more, at a seedy little club called Budland on Chicago's South Side. One time, he took along the novelist Nelson Algren; the other, Terkel brought his wife. He remembers Holiday singing "Strange Fruit" and "Willow, Weep for Me," and thinking how, by revealing her own vulnerability, a great artist makes everyone else feel vulnerable, too. "There were twenty people in the audience, eighteen blacks and two whites, and we were all bawling," he said.

Whenever Terkel talks about "Strange Fruit," he jumps directly to the last line. "The voice goes up—crah-ah-OP!—like a scream," he said. "It's like that painting by Munch of the woman screaming, only in this case, you hear it. She leaves the last note hanging. And then—bang!—it ends. That's it. The body drops. I don't know of any other song, jazz or pop, that has that kind of ending." Only one other composition, he said, is powerful in the same way; "Der Leiermann," the finale of the Schubert cycle "Winterreise," in which a despondent lover, at the brink of death or madness himself, encounters an elderly, barefoot hurdy-gurdy man shivering in the cold, and asks him to play his sad songs.

Even in ostensibly safe locales, "Strange Fruit" wasn't always well received. "Lots of people walked out on the song, party after party, because they said 'we don't call this entertainment,' " Josephson once said. "I remember a time a woman followed Billie into the powder room. Billie was wearing a strapless gown and she tried to brush the woman off. The woman became hysterical with tears—'*Don't you sing that song again! Don't you dare!*' she screamed—and ripped Billie's [dress]. I asked her to leave. She started to cry again. She explained she came to Café Society to have fun and here she heard Billie sing about 'burning flesh' and it brought back a lynching she had seen when she was seven or eight years old down South. She saw a black man tied by the throat to a back fender of a car, dragged through the streets, hung up and burned. She thought she forgot it and Billie brought it back."

Hounded by the red-baiting of J. Edgar Hoover and his covey of favored columnists and facing competition from other clubs, Josephson had unloaded both the uptown and downtown versions of Café Society by the early 1950s. Some other New York clubs refused to let Holiday sing "Strange Fruit," prompting her to specify by contract that she could perform it if she chose. That still didn't guarantee anything. A patron at Jimmy Ryan's on West 52nd Street once requested it, only to see Holiday come back afterward almost in tears. "Did you hear that bartender ringing the cash register all through?" she asked him. "He always does that when I sing."

"Strange Fruit" has "a way of separating the straight people from the squares and cripples," Holiday said in her autobiography. She recalled the time a woman in Los Angeles asked her to sing "that sexy song" she was so famous for, "you know, the one about the naked bodies swinging in the trees." (She said she refused.) Another time, at a club outside Los Angeles (where Lana Turner regularly asked her to perform it), a young white man hurled racial epithets at her. "After two shows of this I was ready to quit," she later recalled. "I knew if I didn't, the third time round I might bounce something off that cracker and land in some San Fernando ranch-type jail." Instead, Bob Hope, who was at the club with Judy Garland, badgered the heckler until he left.

In interviews, Holiday said that whenever she performed "Strange Fruit" in the South there was trouble. She told one newspaper that she was driven out of Mobile, Alabama, for trying to sing it. In fact, while Holiday did appear in Mobile, she made few Southern tours and there's little evidence she sang "Strange Fruit" very often when she did. Stories of jukeboxes offering "Strange Fruit" down South being smashed seem fanciful, if only because Commodore records didn't circulate that far—at least not until Decca started distributing them several years later. The song *did* make jukeboxes in Southern PXs—stores on military bases—patronized primarily by black GIs. "Black soldiers were more aware of that song, because they were in service to their country and yet there were lynchings going on," said Ed Lee, a former GI who heard "Strange Fruit" at the PX near Hendricks Field in Seebring, Florida. "The song was a topic of frequent conversation."

Claims that "Strange Fruit" was banned on the radio are equally hard to document but not hard to believe; radio stations played few records then (the first reported use of the term "disc jockey" does not occur until 1941) and rarely anything controversial. The producers of nationally broadcast programs like "The Lucky Strike Hit Parade" or "The Make-Believe Ballroom" played little jazz, and when they did, they were far more likely to feature the Ink Spots or Cab Calloway than Billie Holiday singing "Strange Fruit." "I don't think it was ever banned officially," said pianist and jazz expert Billy Taylor, who heard Holiday perform "Strange Fruit" at the Howard Theater in Washington. "I think they just said, 'Don't play that.' "

Even in ostensibly open-minded New York, putting the song on the air was an iffy proposition. Radio host Alan Courtney—who earned a bit of anonymous immortality in 1941 for writing the lyrics to "Joltin' Joe DiMaggio"—played the song on a station, now defunct, called WOV. But elsewhere on the dial, all was timidity. "WNEW has been trying to get up the courage to allow Billie Holiday, singing at Café Society, to render the anti-lynching song—'Strange Fruit Growing on the Trees Down South'—on one of the night spot's regular broadcasts," the *New York Post* reported in November 1939. "Station turned thumbs down a week ago, but approved the number for last night's airing. Then it said 'no' again, but has agreed to let Billie sing it tonight at one o'clock." "Strange Fruit" was also banned on the BBC. But given the song's message, it effectively kept itself off the air, with or without edicts. "It was a downer," Milt Gabler recalled.

Holmes "Daddy-O" Daylie did play "Strange Fruit" regularly, at least when given the chance. "I would play it when I felt like it, sometimes two or three times a month, because it gave a message," he said. "If there was some racial event—say, a racist cop that beat a black youngster for running a red light—and there was an uproar in the community, I might write a little commentary and play 'Strange Fruit.' They used to call me a rabble-rouser." He said that people were forever requesting the song so they could tape it and play it for friends. He was able to oblige them while working for small, independent stations, where getting clearance was never much of a problem. But when Daylie moved to the mighty WGN, the radio station of the *Chicago Tribune*, which could be heard in forty states, he managed to get it on the air only a couple of times a year. "I couldn't play it too often because they got some negative feedback," he said.

"Strange Fruit" never penetrated many regions of the American consciousness. "Most Middle-America white swing fans never heard it and went on discovering Glenn Miller instead," the musicologist Gunther Schuller has written. Among blacks, too, the song reverberated mostly among the intelligentsia, and the older intelligentsia at that. "Kids in black colleges were unhappy with the song," recalled Frank Bolden of the *Pittsburgh Courier*, the most prominent newspaper in the then-thriving black press. "They thought these kinds of songs made fun of black people."

"It wasn't a pop hit," said Ahmet Ertegun. "The man in

the street wasn't aware of it. People on 125th Street [in Harlem] didn't know what the song was about or the existence of the song, but black intellectuals were very much affected by it."

In the black newspapers, references to "Strange Fruit" were rare, muted, strangely off-key. Every move of performers like Ella Fitzgerald and Marian Anderson was minutely chronicled; Holiday was largely left alone, perhaps because she was "trouble." "Billie Holiday, buxom blues singer at New York's swank Café Society night club in Sheridan Square, is now heard in what is believed to be the first phonograph recording in America of a popular song that has lynching as its theme," the *New York Age*, a black-owned weekly, reported in a small front-page story in June 1939. "By all means get a load of [Holiday's] recording of 'Strange Fruit,' " the *Amsterdam News* urged the following month, "and although you'd never guess from the title, it is a swell bit of propaganda against lynching." (A few months later, the paper reported that this "anti-lynching monotonic chant" helped put "umph" in Holiday's Café Society appearances.) Frank Marshall Davis, official "discographer" of the Associated Negro Press, listed "Strange Fruit" among the notable records of 1939, but almost offhandedly, as the flip side of "Fine and

Mellow." "The coupling 'Strange Fruit,' the only thing of its type ever recorded, is equally interesting," he blandly stated.

Albert Murray, the eminent historian of the blues and jazz, said that "Strange Fruit" "had a bigger moral or sentimental impact among white liberals, mainly Northern liberals and do-gooders," than it had among blacks, Northern or, particularly, Southern. "They probably didn't pay any attention to it in Georgia; 'Blue and Sentimental' by Count Basie was the big hit that year," he said. "You don't celebrate New Year's over chitlins and Champagne with 'Strange Fruit.' You don't get next to someone playing 'Strange Fruit.' Who the hell wants to go hear something that reminds them of a lynching?"

Some African-Americans, like Paul Robeson, disliked the song because it portrayed blacks as victims. Others literally feared the song, thinking that far from enlightening people, it would stir up racial hatreds and actually lead to a new wave of lynchings. "Miss Holiday recently sang the ballad at the Howard Theatre, Washington," the Baltimore *Afro-American* reported in March 1940, "and speculation became rife as to whether it actually will incite or condemn mob action." (The song, the paper also reported, had "immediately won praise from musical critics of both the hot and the classical schools.") And millions of uneducated rural blacks were either oblivious or uncomprehending. "Unless you interpreted it for the people, they didn't know what it meant," said Frank Bolden of the *Pittsburgh Courier*. "It could have been watermelons growing on the ground."

But for Bolden and other members of the black elite, the song was almost sacred. Listening to it, he recalled, "was like sitting in church. It was like a hymn to us." Indeed, the civil rights establishment paid heed. Walter White of the NAACP praised the singer and the song. "The music is very beautiful and Miss Holiday sings this piece with extraordinary power," he said. Bolden recalls that White, anxious to prod other black performers into speaking out against racial injustice, sent Holiday a letter—reprinted in the *Courier*—congratulating her for the song. "Duke Ellington and Cab Calloway and Count Basie and Jimmie Lunceford and the rest did not become active civil rights participants," Bolden said. "What [White] was really trying to do was to get people like Duke into the campaign." Lester Granger of the Urban League also praised Holiday. Bolden speculated that Holiday might even have won the NAACP's prestigious Spingarn Medal, given annually to blacks for special achievements, had the black church not disapproved of entertainers at the time.

Clearly, "Strange Fruit" came nowhere near to selling one million records, as the *Amsterdam News* reported in September 1944, and much of what it did sell was due to "Fine and Mellow." But the record's success did not go unnoticed at Columbia. According to one source, it emboldened the label to record Holiday's other famously dark tune, "Gloomy Sunday," which was banned from the airwaves for a very different reason: it supposedly led people to commit suicide.

Holiday did sing "Strange Fruit" for large black audiences. In 1943, for instance, she performed it at a benefit for Ben Davis, Jr., a black man elected as a Communist to the New York City Council. (Paul Robeson, Teddy Wilson, Josh White, Ella Fitzgerald, and Hazel Scott participated in the same event.) She also sang it several times at the famed Apollo Theater in Harlem. Jack Schiffman, whose family ran the Apollo, said his father initially did not want Holiday to perform it there, fearing that it would lead to disturbances. But in his memoirs, Schiffman described what happened when she finally did.

"If you heard it done anywhere else you might have been touched and nothing more," he wrote. "But at the Apollo the song took on profound intimations. Not only did you see the 'fruit' evoked in all its graphic horror, but

1. Billie Holiday performing at Café Society, 1939.

2. *New Yorker* ad, 1939.

3. The lynching of Thomas Shipp and Abram Smith,
August 7, 1930, Marion, Indiana.

4. The lynching of Rubin Stacy, July 19, 1935, Fort Lauderdale, Florida.

Strange Record

Billie Holiday is a roly-poly young colored woman with a hump in her voice. Dance-hall crowds have heard her with Count Basie's Orchestra, radio audiences with Artie Shaw. She does not care enough about her figure to watch her diet, but she loves to sing. She also likes to listen to records of her singing.

Last spring Billie Holiday went to the Manhattan studios of the Vocalion Company, which has her under exclusive contract, to make a batch of records. One number, which she had been singing at a new downtown hotspot called Café Society, she particularly wanted on wax. Called *Strange Fruit,* it had been written by a libertarian New York public school teacher named Lewis Allan and its lyric was a poetic description of a lynching's terrible finale. Billie liked its dirge-like blues melody, was not so much interested in the song's social content. But Vocalion was. The record was never made.

Last week Manhattan's Commodore Music Shop—which not only makes and sells records but provides loafing room for most of the city's hot musicians—gave Billie and others a chance to hear her sing *Strange Fruit,* and also provided the National Association for the Advancement of Colored People a prime piece of musical propaganda. Unsqueamish, the Commodore had not balked at recording Teacher Allan's grim and gripping lyrics, which begin:

Southern trees bear a strange fruit,
Blood on the leaves and blood at the root,
Black bodies swinging in the Southern breeze,
Strange fruit hanging from the poplar trees. . . .

5. This 1939 *Time* article accompanied a photograph of Holiday, one that Café Society owner Barney Josephson later claimed was the first photograph of a black person in the pages of a mainstream magazine.

6. Barney Josephson, proprietor of Café Society, c. 1939.

7. Milt Gabler beams with pride in front of his Commodore Records display window.

8. Promotional poster for Billie Holiday concert
at Carnegie Hall, 1954.

9. Billie at the Apollo accompanied by pianist Art Tatum, January 1944.

10. Robin Carson portrait of
Billie Holiday, 1944.

11. Holiday (center) observes friends jamming at a private party at the
studio of Hearst newspaper political cartoonist Burris Jenkins, August
1939. From left: trombonist J. C. Higginbotham, bassist Clyde Newcombe,
trumpeter Rex Stewart, Billie, record producer Harry Lim, Eddie Condon,
trumpeter Max Kaminsky, trumpeter Hot Lips Page—and on the drums,
Cozy Cole.

12. Billie Holiday performs late in her career, 1950s.

you saw in Billie Holiday the wife or sister or mother of one of the victims beneath the tree, almost prostrate with sorrow and fury. . . . Perhaps, if your orientation was such—as it surely was for Apollo audiences—you even saw and felt the agony of another lynching victim, this one suspended from a wooden cross at Calvary. And when she wrenched the final words from her lips, there was not a soul in that audience, black or white, who did not feel half-strangled. A moment of oppressively heavy silence followed, and then a kind of rustling sound I had never heard before. It was the sound of almost two thousand people sighing."

Before long, "Strange Fruit" took on other permutations. In the 1940s, Jerome Robbins choreographed a duet for himself and Anita Alvarez to the song. Around the same time, the dancer Pearl Primus, who also appeared at Café Society, created a similar work, in which Primus, who was black, played a white woman witnessing a lynching. Though the dance was not set to the song, she called it "Strange Fruit."

Shortly before her death in 1994, Primus told David Gere, who teaches dance history and theory at UCLA, of a lunch with Holiday and Meeropol in 1943 in which Holiday somehow revealed that the song's message had eluded

her. "I said, 'What do you *think* they're talking about?' "
Primus recalled asking her. "Afterwards I thought, 'My
God, how could this woman sing this thing and not know
the facts?' " Politics and protests weren't Holiday's métier,
she concluded; when Billie Holiday sang "Strange Fruit,"
she was acting. Primus's story seems unconvincing; for
one thing, Meeropol never mentioned such an encounter.

Measured strictly by the number of his performances,
the span of time over which he performed it, and the ag-
gregate size of his audiences, Josh White arguably popu-
larized "Strange Fruit" as much as Holiday did. His
connection to the material was even more immediate:
While leading blind black street singers around the South
as a child, he'd actually happened upon a lynching. White
never forgot the scene of drunken whites and their rowdy
children cavorting as two black men hung from trees;
from time to time, he said, the merrymakers jabbed the
two victims in the testicles with hot branding irons.

White's version of "Strange Fruit" is intense, almost
febrile, but it is less searing and subtle than Holiday's.
"When Josh sings it, you feel you're hearing a great per-
formance," said White's biographer, Elijah Wald. "When
Billie sings it, you feel as if you're at the foot of the tree."
(The comparison brings to mind what the clarinetist
Tony Scott once said about Holiday and the other First

Lady of Song, Ella Fitzgerald: "With a singer like Ella, when she sings 'my man has left me,' you think the guy's going down the street for a loaf of bread. But when Lady sings it, man, you see the bags are packed, the cat's going down the street, and *you know he ain't never coming back!*") Still, White told friends he felt Holiday's version lacked conviction because, as someone who'd spent most of her time in Northern cities, she couldn't possibly identify with the trauma of lynching.

Like Holiday, White made a ritual out of performing "Strange Fruit," saving it for last, insisting on quiet. He, too, encountered plenty of hostility. When he introduced the song in New Castle, Pennsylvania, a man in the audience shouted, "Yeah, that song was written by a nigger lover!" and headed menacingly toward the stage.

White said that he was asked to perform the song as often in the South as in the North. But he was singing it years later than Holiday, and usually on college campuses. Shelby Foote, later the famous Civil War historian, heard White sing it at Café Society, and found the whole thing a bit heavy-handed. "I resented the utter caricature of it," he recalled. So he playfully urged White afterwards to come down to Mississippi and try it out there. ("It was a cruel thing to say," he confessed.) "Man, you must be joking," White replied.

Brigitte McCulloch Remembers

Brigitte McCulloch, who'd grown up in war-torn Hamburg, came to Chicago in 1957, the twenty-year-old bride of a GI: "I'd left behind a still-aching Germany with all its guilt and confusion and taboos to embrace this vibrant, confident, and comfortingly normal country," she recalled. "My own baggage of horrid memories and guilt became lighter in time until I could almost forget." Then, two experiences, occurring at roughly the same time, helped her to begin confronting, and contending with, her past. First, she looked down upon the arm of a man selling her a piece of fabric, and she saw a number tattooed on it. She was dumbfounded, ashamed, utterly unsure what to do. Then, she tuned in to a radio program on WFMT in Chicago called "Midnight Special," and heard Josh White sing "Strange Fruit."

Suddenly, she realized she had to grapple with her own past, or at least her family's and her nation's. "On those Southern trees, along with the black men, hung the murdered Jews, hung all of the victims of violence," she said. "And one survived to tell the story, to tear our hearts apart, to make us feel and remember."

✍

White told of a Southern military officer who stalked out of one performance of "Strange Fruit," only to return, conscience-stricken, a week later to force himself to hear it. The man then came back a third time with his wife and invited White to join them—the first time the woman had ever shared a table with a black man. Concert-goers recall women from the states of the Old Confederacy sobbing while White sang the song, and apologizing to him afterward for all of the sins of the South.

For his troubles, White was hauled before the House Un-American Activities Committee in 1950. "Why shouldn't a Negro artist—and for that matter any decent person—raise his voice against lynching?" he asked the committee. "My records of this song have sold big," he added. "If they helped make my fellow Americans more aware of the evil, I am pleased." But always, he said, he took care to follow it with Meeropol's ode to America, "The House I Live In." And when he went to Europe he, unlike Holiday, refused to perform it, even though it was what people invariably wanted to hear. "It's one thing to complain of lynching in America, where your listeners know that it does not detract from your loyalty and love for your country," he explained. "It seemed to me quite another to complain of it abroad, where the listeners might think it's the whole story."

Occasionally, others performed the song. For instance, Laura Duncan, who'd sung it before Holiday had, dusted it off for rallies during the 1948 presidential campaign of Progressive Party candidate Henry Wallace, to which left-wingers—unhappy with President Harry S. Truman and New York Governor Thomas E. Dewey—flocked. On a few occasions, in New York and Connecticut, George Wein, the impresario who later created the Newport Jazz Festival, accompanied her on the piano.

Sometimes perfection happens, and this was one of those times . . . the perfect horror described in a voice which could encompass horror without apparent effort or strain, making it far more indelible than the dramatic emphasis of opera. . . . Still, I have to wonder if she truly understood the power of "Strange Fruit." To bring into the world of swinging, light-hearted or blues-like jazz a song about the deepest shame of racist America was like inviting your neighborhood murderer to your Fourth of July barbecue and expecting your friends to accept him as just another guest, and the occasion as just another day in their lives.

—*Frances Rowe, jazz aficionado, who heard Holiday perform in San Francisco in the late 1950s*

Sometimes perfection happens

D RUGS AND ALCOHOL had been part of Holi-
day's life for years—between sets at Café Society,
she would routinely smoke marijuana in a cab riding
around Central Park—but only in the early 1940s did she
begin taking heroin, then mainlining it. That, plus the
death of her mother and a series of disastrous relation-
ships with abusive men, sent her life into a desperate,
downward spiral. In the spring of 1947 she checked into a
New York hospital for detoxification (a nurse was among
several people who supposedly supplied her with drugs
there) and within a few months she was busted in
Philadelphia, spending nearly a year in a federal peniten-

tiary in Pennsylvania. (Before her first day was out, she had gotten high again).

Still, as much as she abused herself, as erratic and unreliable as she became, she could still perform memorably, even miraculously. "All you ever saw was this incredible face in a pool of light that completely mesmerized the audience from the moment she got on the floor to the moment she left it," the singer Sylvia Syms recalled. "And no matter where it was, no matter whatever distance, wherever, from a balcony seat in Carnegie Hall or close to the bar in the Rendezvous Lounge in the Senator Hotel in Philadelphia years ago, in the Onyx Club or Three Deuces—wherever you saw her, and I went to see her everywhere possible—you saw the world in that face. You saw everything that was human, everything that was alive, all the beauty and misery of life. There was an aura about this face that was celestial and otherworldly."

And wherever, whenever Billie Holiday sang "Strange Fruit," it was an event. "Miss Holiday has a style particularly suited to her famous lament 'Strange Fruit Hangs on Southern Trees,' without which no appearance of this singer is complete," the *New York Sun* reported in 1944. The novelist Paul Bowles, then music critic for the *New York Herald Tribune*, heard Holiday at her legendary concert at New York's Town Hall in 1946. "As usual, she sang

'Strange Fruit,' a piece which never fails to get a huge hand," he wrote. In *PM*, the legendarily innovative and progressive (but short-lived) New York daily, Seymour Peck reviewed some of the songs on Holiday's program. "Through them all," he wrote, "Miss Holiday maintained her usual personal austerity, her refusal to distract the listener from her music with tricks of 'personality.' For her, the voice conveys all. The knee marking time beneath her shimmering gown, the ringed fingers snapping now and then—these serve only to help her keep rhythm. And even these were abandoned when Miss Holiday sang the tragic, haunted 'Strange Fruit.' "

The *New York Times* described another concert at Carnegie Hall two years later, shortly after her release from prison. " 'Strange Fruit,' her most famous number, was heard in utter silence, but with intense applause at the end," it reported. "Throat-tightening" was how *Time* described the song on the same occasion.

Gene Marine Remembers

Gene Marine was a 22-year-old off-and-on college student when he heard Holiday at another Café Society, this one a largely black club in the Fillmore District of San Francisco, in the late 1940s. She'd suddenly gone into "Strange Fruit" that night, and the room went instantly quiet. He was surprised; he had heard that she no longer performed it in public. As Holiday sang, Marine turned away from her momentarily and spotted his waitress. Moments before, she'd been as animated as everyone else in the place. Now, she was leaning against the wall, crying. "There were tears running down her face and she was standing perfectly still," he said. "I remember her standing there, I can even remember what she was wearing, because I was so impressed by that. I've never heard the song since or played the record without thinking of the sight of her."

✍

As many people recount it, whenever Billie Holiday sang "Strange Fruit" she went into a world of her own. That seems to have been what a friend of Holiday's, a young playwright named Greer Johnson, sensed when he arranged to have a portrait photographer named Robin Carson take some publicity shots of Holiday in the mid-1940s. (Johnson, a gay Southern white man who later produced Holiday's Town Hall concert, had already bonded with the singer: "The first recording I heard in Lexington, Kentucky, was 'Strange Fruit,' " he once said, "and I knew then that this was sung by somebody I had to know.") Carson clicked away for hours, but felt he had yet to capture the singer's essence. Holiday, perplexed, asked Johnson what to do, and he ordered her to stand by the fireplace and sing "Strange Fruit." After a bit of protesting—she said she needed an accompanist—Holiday complied, performing it a cappella. "It was one of the most fantastic performances I have ever heard in my life, and [Carson's] camera never stopped," Johnson later recalled. So it is that "Strange Fruit," plus a bottle of gin, produced one of the most famous portraits of Holiday ever taken (see photo insert).

So associated did Holiday become with the song that she claimed nonexistent connections to it. "And now I'd like to sing a tune, it was written especially for me, it's titled 'Strange Fruit,'" she said during a "Jazz at the Philharmonic" concert in 1945, later released on record. With every indignity she suffered, her passion for the song seemed to grow. In 1944, for instance, Holiday lost a gig in St. Louis for fraternizing with a white man; the experience highlighted, according to the *Amsterdam News*, "why she sings 'Strange Fruit' with so much fervor and smoldering hatred in her eyes."

And with every defeat she suffered, with every additional increment of abuse she endured or inflicted upon herself, the more personal the song came to seem. The confidence with which she'd first sung it gave way to pure pathos. Watching her undertake it could be both exhilarating and excruciating. "I can still remember vividly the tingling of my spine as she sang 'strange fruit hangin' from the poplar trees,' " recalled Humphrey Noyes, a graduate student at Columbia after World War II. "And I felt something akin to the twisting of my heart in real agony as she so inimitably ended with her drawn-out soul cry of 'a strange and bitter crop.' These, for me, were the most memorable words I ever heard in all my years of listening to jazz and the blues. Utterly haunting."

Holiday performed "Strange Fruit," but she rationed those performances. When the setting wasn't right to her—say, in a nightclub filled with revelers—she declined the inevitable requests, no matter how insistent, or tacked it on to the end of her last show, when the house was down to a few stalwarts. "I said to her, 'Lady, why don't you ever do this when you have your crowds? Why don't you do this more often?' " Daddy-O Daylie reminisced. "I'll never forget it: she said, 'I only do it for people who might understand and appreciate it. This is not a "June-Moon-Croon-Tune." This song tells a story about pain and heartache.' She would look at the people and if they didn't look as if they were really hip she wouldn't do the tune. They had to meet her approval." Afterward, there would be no more encores. "Miss Holiday never sings anything, *anything*, after 'Strange Fruit,' " the master of ceremonies at one San Francisco nightclub sternly told patrons there.

Indeed, when Holiday called for "Strange Fruit," the evening was over—sometimes even before it began. The pianist Jimmy Rowles remembered one night in Billy Berg's Trouville Club in Los Angeles when the singer, drunk and freshly beaten by her husband, was surly by the time she reached the stage. "As she slowly makes her way to the end of the bar, she's got ten more feet and if we can just get her past she's okay. But all of a sudden— twelve blasts later—she gets into an argument with a cat. She curses the son-of-a-bitch motherfucker—boom!— and stomps away. And now she's madder than a bitch, she's out of her skull and by the time she gets up on the bandstand, she hates the world, it's like the atomic bomb that destroyed Hiroshima, she doesn't like it at all. [The pianist Bobby] Tucker's waiting for her and she turns to him and says 'Strange Fruit.' Only 'Strange Fruit' means the end of the show, it's like the last tune she sings. Bobby says 'But, Lady . . .' and Lady turns around and slams the thing [piano] down and Bobby barely gets his hands away as it goes—bam!—down and he could have lost them at the wrists. He looks at me and—whew!—he mops his brow and she has one hand on the edge of the piano and she says again, 'Strange Fruit.' He says 'Okay, Lady,' and does 'Strange Fruit,' and she walks off the stage after one fucking tune. And all those money motherfuckers have been sitting out there three hours waiting for her in their fur coats and their Beverly Hills bullshit, spending their bread, but this is a fact and all the cats will back me up: they still loved her, they all loved her."

Decades later, the experience of listening to, and watching, Billie Holiday perform "Strange Fruit"—her eyes closed and head back, the familiar gardenia over her ear, her ruby lipstick magnifying her mocha complexion, her fingers snapping lightly, her hands holding the microphone stand as if it were a teacup—lingered in many memories. "You could not look away—not for a moment," said Kenneth Miller, who had just finished a thesis at Stanford on the economics of slavery when he heard her in San Jose in 1950. The actress Billie Allen Henderson recalled how, during Holiday's appearance at New York's Birdland in 1952, the maître d' actually confiscated all cigarettes before Holiday began singing it. "I was standing there with my date when she started singing this song," she recalled. "I was trying to be sophisticated and all of a sudden something stabs me in the solar plexus and I was gasping for air. It was so deeply felt. I understood it. I understood it. I could smell the burning flesh; I felt it. She was . . . unrelenting is a good word for it. Some didn't know how to react. They weren't quite sure. Nobody stirred. It was startling, and I'll never forget it. I thought, 'That's what art can do.' "

Dempsey Travis, a former jazz musician and author of several books, heard a decrepit, dissipated Holiday sing it several times on Chicago's South Side. "The words told the story but her face never reflected any emotion," he said. "You listened to every word; it was like watching water drop slowly from a faucet. It was as if she was singing 'Ave Maria' or 'Amazing Grace.' "

Fred Stone, then newly discharged from the navy, watched her reluctantly perform the song for a group of naval officers in 1946 at Chicago's Garrick Stage Bar, where she was appearing with Red Allen's band and the trombonist J. C. Higginbotham. "I could see tears on the face of J. C. Higginbotham," he said. "When she finished there was no applause, but everyone in the club just stood up with their heads bowed. It was one of the most moving experiences of my life."

But Holiday's problems increasingly lent the experience extra poignancy and, sometimes, revulsion. Around the time Stone heard Holiday in Chicago, another World War II veteran, Saul Lassoff, saw her on 52nd Street in

New York. Minutes after watching her on the stage, Lassoff spotted Holiday approaching the bar with a huge dog on a leash. "I was so flabbergasted seeing her and said something silly like 'Billie, you are great.' What caused me to have mixed emotions was her dribbling back something unintelligible—the words just dribbled out—and I couldn't believe this was the same person I had just viewed. She was obviously under the effects of heroin or some drug, which she must have shot up on after her singing. I'll never forget the effect on me: both adulation and disgust is what I felt."

Dorothy Vella Remembers

Dorothy Vella, an editor and jazz buff, heard Billie Holiday perform "Strange Fruit" in San Francisco in the early 1950s. (It was not the first time; she'd seen her in Washington, D.C., a bit earlier: "All of us sat as if stunned, immobilized by the intensity of our emotion. I think we felt as if we had seen more deeply into another person's suffering than we had any right to see . . . it took us at least a quarter of an hour to regain our composure sufficiently to talk to our companions in a natural manner again.") In San Francisco, too, Vella recalls, a hush fell over the crowd as Holiday began. "But a few seconds later the spell was broken by noise from a table in the center of the room where there were several couples in a celebratory mood. One of the men began to rise from his seat, wave his arms in the air, and call loudly for a waitress to bring him another Scotch. Billie stopped singing immediately. She stared at the man for a few seconds, then said, very coldly, 'I'll have to stop. If you're going to talk during this song, I just won't sing it.' Then she began to walk out of the spotlight. Some people in the audience began to object, to urge Billie to reconsider. And one of the tablemates of the offending man pushed him down in his seat and told him, very sharply, to be quiet. He obeyed meekly, and when it became clear that he was not going to cause any more trouble, Billie did reconsider. She nodded, returned to the spotlight, gave a signal to her pianist, and slowly started over again. This time, all of the members of the audience were absolutely silent. And at the end of her performance, we all continued to sit very still—deeply thoughtful, profoundly moved. Was there ever a song that was more powerfully charged with emotion? It was actually painful to hear Billie sing that song. It is now almost fifty years since I heard her sing 'Strange Fruit,' but I can still see and hear

*her singing about that 'strange and bitter crop'; her voice
still haunts me."*

～

The song's popularity extended to Europe, where Holiday—evidently not sharing Josh White's concern about appearing "unpatriotic" or of being hauled before the House Un-American Activities Committee herself—performed it several times during a 1954 tour. If anything, it went down more easily there, partly because fans there did not take it personally or defensively. "In America no one would say anything and they'd try to look like they didn't hear the song," said the pianist Mal Waldron. "It was a little embarrassing for Americans to hear it." After Holiday sang "Strange Fruit" at Royal Albert Hall in London, a British reviewer called the song "a challenge to humanity which cannot leave any right-thinking man or woman unaffected." The *Chicago Defender* reported: "They would not let her go until she shook the rafters of this Royal edifice . . . with her soul-disturbing, dramatic rendition of *'Strange Fruit.'* The crowd hung on to her every syllable, to every nuance of Billie's indescribably moving voice."

But the politics of "Strange Fruit" sometimes eluded foreign audiences. At the Concertgebouw in Amsterdam, the audience laughed as Holiday sang the song, and she stormed off the stage. (Afterward, some Dutch newspapers scolded the master of ceremonies, Leonard Feather, for not explaining the song beforehand.) And where the song was understood, it could still prove unsettling, at least if Meeropol's attempt to record a French translation by Henri-Jacques Dupuy is any indication. "Although I have shown '*Étrange Fruit*' to many French performers, it has not been possible to have a recording scheduled on your tune," Parisian song publisher Rudi Rével wrote Meeropol in 1955. "The main reason . . . is the political angle of the French version which is almost considered here as frankly anti-American." Rével then offered a second, more compelling, explanation for his difficulties, one that must have proven powerful in the era of Dien Bien Phu and the war in Algeria. "With all the troubles the French are currently having with coloured people in Indochina and North Africa, I do not think it will be possible to get a major recording of Mr. Dupuy's version," he noted.

I remember the first time [bassist] Red [Callender] played a record of Billie: "Strange Fruit." I said, "What is that, man?" That may have been why they were against her, too . . . exposing discrimination, putting it on stage. . . . That's when I changed my idea of a song telling a story. That music is here to tell the white world the wrongs they done in race.

—*Bassist Charles Mingus*

telling a story

F AMED PRODUCER Norman Granz was militant
on civil rights issues, such as lynching. He later said
that Holiday's experiences at the Trouville Club in Los
Angeles—where, she complained to him, her black
friends were barred from her appearances—impelled
him to take the lead desegregating the jazz business. But
he said that he would only ask Holiday to sing "Strange
Fruit" when she was in reasonably good spirits; it would
have been unfair were she already down in the dumps.

But as Mal Waldron remembers it, it was precisely
when she was depressed that she would add it to her pro-
gram. "Whenever things were not going right, she would
sing that tune—if the dressing room wasn't too beautiful

or maybe the police were waiting outside and stopped her or something like that," he said. Sometimes, she would turn to it to punish audiences, to chasten them for their inattentiveness. "She would get herself together to do that one," Waldron said. "The others were kind of natural tunes and she would spin them off the way she talked. This one was special. She had to do preparation for this one. There was a certain willful purpose when she sang that tune."

After two versions for Commodore, Holiday went on to record "Strange Fruit" four more times. The first was at the "Jazz at the Philharmonic" concert in 1945; it is starker and bleaker than the original—"most powerful of all is 'Strange Fruit,' on which Billie breaks into an unashamed sob," *Down Beat* reported in a review—and the way in which she clears her throat three times before starting seems either a sign of her declining health or a portent of the problems to come. There is also a recording made at George Wein's Boston nightclub, Storyville, in 1951; a studio version from 1956; and a telecast from London in February 1959. None of these later recordings matches the purity and understated eloquence of the original. "I recorded more sides of Billie than anyone else, and I can't recall that she ever asked me to record it. And it never occurred to me to give it to anyone else, say Ella," said Norman Granz, who produced Ella Fitzgerald's famous "songbooks" for Verve.

Toward the end of her life, Holiday seems to have performed the song a bit less often. Partly it took too much out of her; she was too busy holding herself together to wage crusades for anybody else. "She didn't like to sing it because it hurt her so much. She would cry every time she would do it," said Lee Young, the drummer and brother of Lester Young, the legendary saxophonist who dubbed Holiday "Lady Day." Partly, it was that not everyone wanted to hear it, including the musicians playing behind her. ("I had enough of that living in Louisiana and Texas. I was trying to get away from that," said Illinois Jacquet, who played tenor saxophone behind her in the 1950s.) Partly it was the climate of the times: the country no longer wanted shrill songs of social protest. " 'Fine and Mellow' was a friendly, happy encore, so unlike the 'Strange Fruit' that so often used to serve that function," Bill Coss wrote in *Metronome* in 1952. "Perhaps this is an indication of the new Holiday. Certainly it was a real holiday for me." Partly, it was that the song still led to unpleasantness, like when she'd included it in her first set on opening night in a Miami nightclub in 1956. "Billie, singing this great number with unusual emphasis, wasn't surprised that about seven couples walked out on her—

but the majority of fans stayed and applauded," the *Pittsburgh Courier* reported. (The management nonetheless asked her not to sing it again.) For all the times he watched her, Holiday's last lawyer, Earle Zaidins, said he never heard her perform "Strange Fruit" at all.

Morgan Monceaux Remembers

One day in the late 1950s, several white men in a small town in Louisiana began taunting a young black boy named Morgan Monceaux. "Nigger!" they shouted at him. Profoundly shocked by what was his first real brush with racism, Monceaux went home and told his grandmother what had just happened. "She said, 'There's something that you need to hear,' and she put on this record of Billie Holiday singing 'Strange Fruit,' " recalled Monceaux, now an artist in Rhode Island. "And then she walked away. It was up to me to come to my own conclusions. We never talked about it after that. She assumed that after hearing that, I realized what was going on. I started listening to that song and said 'Whoa!' I played it over and over to get a better perspective on what type of world I was living in. I play it a lot now. It helps me understand that there are

ignorant people in the world, and it allows me to have
pity for their ignorance."

✍

Holiday's autobiography appeared in 1956. In it, as the biographer Linda Kuehl once put it, Holiday "bent the truth as she might bend a note to give it extra verve." Meeropol complained about the misinformation it contained on "Strange Fruit," and won a pledge from the publisher, Doubleday, to fix all the mistakes. To buttress his case, he collected affidavits from, among others, Barney Josephson, who called Holiday's claims of partial authorship of "Strange Fruit" "a figment of her imagination." (The mistakes have nonetheless crept back into later editions.)

Though angry about Holiday's revisionist history, Meeropol was charitable to Holiday herself. "Billie Holiday had a problem with liquor and drugs and like other black artists had in many ways a tragic life and a hard road to travel," he once wrote. "I can understand the psychological reasons why the peripheral truths and actual facts surrounding her life were unimportant to her and why she took liberties with them or invented some of them out of whole cloth. . . . I did not hold any enmity toward Billie Holiday for her lapses into fancy nor would

I want the fact that she made untrue statements bruited about now that she is dead."

Holiday sang "Strange Fruit" during an evening of "Jazz Under the Stars" in Central Park in July 1957, but barely managed to get the song out. "She looked stewed, she looked awful," jazz buff Joseph Adams recalled. "I thought, 'I'm looking at a dead woman. She's not long for this world.' She just croaked it out. She'd totally lost her voice." Around the same time, a jazz fan in Berkeley, California, named Frances Rowe saw Holiday, her gown hanging from her like borrowed clothes, at the Blackhawk Club in San Francisco. As usual, Holiday was besieged with requests. But much as she loved "Strange Fruit," Rowe dared not ask Holiday to sing it: it was about death, and she could see that Holiday, who was all of forty-two years old at the time, was approaching death herself.

Holiday performed it again in London in February 1959, in a televised concert that has since been excerpted in several Holiday documentaries. Haggard, largely wasted away, she had grown oddly, sadly suited to capture the full grotesqueness of the song. Now, she not only sang of bulging eyes and twisted mouths. She embodied them.

In *The Heart of a Woman*, Maya Angelou recounts how, during a visit to Los Angeles in 1958, Holiday sang "Strange Fruit" to her young son, Guy.

Billie talked and sang in a hoarse, dry tone the well-known protest song. Her rasping voice and phrasing literally enchanted me. I saw the black bodies hanging from the Southern trees. I saw the lynch victims' blood glide from the leaves down the trunks and onto the roots.

Guy interrupted, "How can there be blood at the root?" I made a hard face and warned him, "Shut up, Guy, just listen." Billie had continued under the interruption, her voice vibrating over harsh edges.

She painted a picture of a lovely land, pastoral and bucolic, then added eyes bulged and mouths twisted, onto the Southern landscape.

Guy broke into her song. "What's a pastoral scene, Miss Holiday?" Billie looked up slowly and studied Guy for a second. Her face became cruel, and when she spoke her voice was scornful. "It means when the crackers are killing the niggers. It means when they take a little nigger like you and snatch off his nuts and shove them down his goddam throat. That's what it means."

The thrust of the rage repelled Guy and stunned me.

Billie continued, "That's what they do. That's a goddam pastoral scene."

✍

Within a year, Holiday was dead.

One day, during my sophomore year in college, a group of us were listening to a Billie Holiday album when she began to sing "Strange Fruit." I had heard it several times before, but it was not until one of the guys said, somewhat startled, "Hey, this song is about hanging Negroes." Then I was both surprised and a bit embarrassed. Why had I not made such an obvious connection sooner? Was my preoccupation with chords and melody causing me to ignore the importance of the lyrics? Perhaps my day-to-day experiences with "segregation de jure" had dulled my senses to the controversial lyrics. I have never been quite sure of the answers.

—*Ellis Marsalis, Jr., jazz musician,*
father of Wynton and Branford

it's so powerful

"STRANGE FRUIT" lived on, but only in a few places. One was in the *People's Songbook,* the collection first put together in 1947 by Pete Seeger and others, from which a few thousand Red Diaper babies faithfully learned the lyrics. People who grew up singing along with the Weavers, Woody Guthrie, Burl Ives, and Paul Robeson learned "Strange Fruit," too.

In the American mainstream, "Strange Fruit" remained too sensitive to sing. According to the folksinger and impresario Bob Gibson, the very prospect petrified the producers of the television folk music program "Hootenanny" in the early 1960s. "So I'm sitting there with Josh

[White] when all of these suits and producer types come over and nervously ask what he was planning to sing," he later said. "He looks at them and says, 'I thought I might do 'Strange Fruit.' They started coughing, sweating, and turning red, and in unison said, 'No! You can't sing that! What else can you sing?' " White could go on the air, or he could sing "Strange Fruit." He could not do both.

Just about the only other major artist to perform the song regularly in the 1960s was Nina Simone. But Simone, whose anger while performing the song was more palpable than Holiday's, came to sing "Strange Fruit" rarely, both because she had her own repertoire of civil rights songs and because, as she once put it, it was "too hard to do."

On the American left, the song became a bit passé. True, the *Boston Globe* invoked it in 1963 when three young civil rights workers, later found murdered, disappeared in Mississippi. But for the young idealists of the civil rights era, the song was simply too depressing or too bitter or too redolent of black victimhood; it was "If I Had a Hammer" and "We Shall Overcome" and "This Little Light of Mine" that buoyed up the Freedom Riders and lunch-counter protesters.

Marc Huestis Remembers

*In his later years, Meeropol was chary of tailoring
"Strange Fruit" to suit new times and locales. "It
belongs to the Thirties and any attempt to 'bring it
up to date' is not only an artistic and social distortion
but an insensitive and foolish one, no matter who
may have suggested it," he once wrote. But in 1977,
a gay theater and film producer named Marc Huestis
created a show called "Strange Fruit," a hybrid offering
of film and poetry performed at San Francisco's Gay
Community Center. The show revised the lyrics of the
original to attack the oppression of "strange fruits,"
that is, nonconformists and outcasts within the gay
community, particularly more effeminate men and drag
queens. ("Here is a fruit for the world to see / For no one
to pick, running wild and free / For no one to tame, for
no one to stop / Here is a strange and bitter crop.")
It met with a mixed reaction. To some gay men, Holiday
was a hero, whose pain seemed kindred to theirs.
That the song referred to "fruit," a slang term the gay
community wished to reclaim from homophobes, only
made it more apt. But to black gays—and some white
ones—the pain of the song was peculiar to blacks*

and the song itself, as Huestis put it, "an anthem that should not be touched." "The strength of passion for this school of thought bordered on the religious," he recalled. "Some also felt that anything a drag queen did was by nature frivolous and funny, and there was no humor to the song."

✍

In 1972 "Strange Fruit" made a cameo appearance in *Lady Sings the Blues*, the movie, whose fictions were even more egregious than anything Holiday had ever cooked up. The film shows Diana Ross as Holiday encountering a lynching while touring the South; stricken by what she sees, she adopts a laser-like, all-knowing look—the look, presumably, of lyrics taking shape. The chords of "Strange Fruit" then sound: a song is born. Apart from reviving old canards about the song's authorship and minting new ones about what Holiday had witnessed, Ross's take on "Strange Fruit" is tinny and utterly unconvincing; its only virtue lies in illustrating the power with which Holiday sang the same song. "It's pretty, but it lacks Holiday's chilling tautness that keeps you silent until the final word, 'crop,' flicks you like a whip," Pauline Kael wrote in *The New Yorker*. "Holiday's acrid edge is missing, and her authority. Ross gives you the phrasing without the intensity that makes it dramatic and memorable, and fresh each time you hear it."

Gil Askey, who put together the music for *Lady Sings the Blues*, put it a bit differently. "Diana Ross is not Billie Holiday; she was an actress singing 'Strange Fruit,' " he said. "In order to sing a song like that, you have to live the hurt Billie Holiday lived in her life. Diana Ross never lived that life."

Far more objectionable than Ross's limited vocal gifts, though, is the censorship. While Ross recorded "Strange Fruit" in its entirety, the film contains only a shortened version of the song. True, the movie was running long, and the film's producers had to hack away at it. But why "Strange Fruit," and why the entire second verse and the first two lines of the third, which contain many of its most powerful images? It may have been that those responsible for the movie—Berry Gordy, Diana Ross, the director Sidney J. Furie, the screenwriters Suzanne De-Passe, Terence McCloy, and Chris Clark—felt that audiences were still not ready for the song. Meeropol, who dismissed the movie as a "thoroughly slick" production in which "shabby, cheap values were substituted for the truth and facts of her life," received $4,500 for the privilege of having his work raped.

By the film's debut Meeropol had long since left teaching and gone into musical composition full time. Between 1944 and 1952 he lived in Hollywood, working for Columbia and MGM; though he was apparently never blacklisted, he once wrote to Dalton Trumbo that he was among those "who felt the hot breath of incipient fascism." By 1952 the Meeropols had returned to New York, where he worked for a time for the NBC television program "The Ford Festival." Though they had never met Ethel and Julius Rosenberg, the Meeropols were in synch with them politically, and offered through a mutual friend to take custody of their two sons, Michael and Robert, while their parents were in jail. The Rosenbergs were executed in June 1953; early the following year, the two boys moved in with the Meeropols, then living in Harlem. An extended court battle followed; at one point, the Society for the Prevention of Cruelty to Children, claiming that the boys "were being exploited for fundraising propositions," convinced a judge in the New York Children's Court to remove them from the Meeropols' care. Michael and Robert were ultimately returned to the Meeropols, who formally adopted them in 1957.

Much of Meeropol's work continued to have political overtones; he wrote the libretto for the opera *The Good Soldier Schweik*, based on an antiwar novel by the Czech novelist Jaroslav Hašek, and worked with Earl Robinson on a cantata based on, of all things, the preamble to the United Nations Charter.

Meeropol developed Alzheimer's disease in the late 1970s; his eldest son played "Strange Fruit" for him in the nursing home, and when the record got too scratchy, he sang it to him. Even after the old man stopped recognizing anyone, he seemed to know the song, and perked up when he heard it. He died of pneumonia in a Jewish nursing home near Springfield, Massachusetts, in 1986, only a few months after Frank Sinatra, by now a Reagan Republican, sang "The House I Live In" at the centennial celebration for the Statue of Liberty. "Strange Fruit" was sung at Meeropol's memorial service. Two weeks after his death, Sting's version of "Strange Fruit" was released on *Rock for Amnesty*, an album to benefit the human rights group Amnesty International.

Kristina Boerger Remembers

In 1998, a lesbian vocal group called Amasong won the GLAMA (Gay and Lesbian American Music Award) for its four-voice, a cappella version of "Strange Fruit." The group, based in Champaign-Urbana, Illinois, is one of several in the lesbian community to perform the song; according to Amasong's director, Kristina Boerger, its appeal in that world reflects both the popularity there of powerful, gender-bending performers like Bessie Smith and Billie Holiday (both of whom had female lovers) and the identification of one historically maligned group with another. "I would not expect a job conducting a choir in the usual church, academic, or civic setting to permit me to program something like 'Strange Fruit,' " she said. "But in the context of gay and lesbian choral movements, this kind of programming is not questioned."

That Amasong—which Boerger describes as "my little, low-budget Midwestern group of rag-tag women, many of whom can't read music and some of whom truly sing badly"—beat out several older and more established groups in the process, says as much about the song itself as about its performance. ("When I heard your recording, I thought: 'Now that is difficult music to sing,' " one contest judge told Boerger afterwards; what he was talking about was not rhythm or notes but "the risk of exposing ourselves to the pain that the song calls forth.") Many lesbian and gay choral directors have asked Boerger for her arrangement. But many more, she believes, have not: they would not have the courage to perform it themselves. "It really requires the performer to look herself / himself square in the face about racism," she said, "and if there were that many white people willing to do that, racism would be lessening."

ᴗᴄ

"Strange Fruit" continued to win popularity around the world. It became well known in Japan, for instance; when Holiday's autobiography was translated there, that was what it was titled. But to some, the song remained too hot to handle. Sometime in the 1980s, a disc jockey in Durham, North Carolina, came across a collection of Billie Holiday standards in the station's library. "Strange Fruit" was circled, with the admonitions "Watch" and "Do not play" printed nearby. And when Robert Meeropol, Abel's younger son, flew on United Airlines a couple of years ago, he noticed that Cassandra Wilson's album *New Moon Daughter* was among the in-flight entertainment, but that its first cut—"Strange Fruit"—was conspicuously missing.

Stephen Reinhardt Remembers

In 1994, Judge Stephen Reinhardt attempted, without success, to convince his colleagues on the United States Court of Appeals in Los Angeles that execution by hanging did not meet evolving societal standards of decency

*and was therefore "cruel and unusual punishment"
prohibited by the United States Constitution. "Hanging
is associated with lynching, with frontier justice, and
with our ugly, nasty, and best-forgotten history of bodies
swinging from the trees or exhibited in public places," he
wrote. He then reached back to a memory from his own
childhood. "To many Americans, judicial hangings call
forth the brutal images of Southern justice immortalized
in a song hauntingly sung by Billie Holiday," he contin-
ued. And in footnote 14 of his opinion, the full text of
"Strange Fruit" appears. "It's one of the two or three
songs that made the greatest impression on me when I
was young, and I never forgot it," Reinhardt later said.
He could have crafted his own broadside against death-
by-hanging, but as far as he was concerned, nothing
captured it better than the song itself. "If I could have
attached as an exhibit a recording of Billie Holiday
singing that song, I would have loved to have done it," he
said.*

✍

The director of the Institute of Jazz Studies at Rutgers
University, Dan Morgenstern, is among those who think
that "Strange Fruit" belongs only to Billie Holiday.
"Frankly, I don't think anybody but Billie should do it," he

said. "I don't think anybody can improve on it." But the song's power and its appeal to a younger generation of performers has grown as the euphoria of the civil rights movement has waned; as the intractability of racial prejudice has become clearer; and as lynching, while no longer a direct threat to most (the murder in 1997 of a black man in Jasper, Texas, being a notable and horrible exception), remains a metaphor for the American black experience. Increasingly, prominent artists have been willing to take it on.

Abbey Lincoln, who tackled "Strange Fruit" on her 1987 album *Abbey Sings Billie*, said she had no trouble singing the song. Slavery's over and so is lynching, she said; her goal was not to dwell on black victimhood but to pay homage to Holiday herself. "She painted a brilliant picture of a horror scene," she said. "It's why I love her so, because she was so honest. She wasn't showing off her voice. She just told us what was going on and it helped to end lynching in the South."

During appearances in Paris in the 1950s Eartha Kitt was asked to sing "Strange Fruit," usually by Americans. Perhaps, she theorized, they figured it was a song all black performers knew. She shied away from it for many years; it brought back too many painful memories of South Carolina, where she'd grown up watching chain gangs and was told never to look a white person in the face. Only when she portrayed Billie Holiday in a one-person show in the 1980s did she perform it. "I could hardly get through it," she recalled. "And it was not only upsetting to me, but I found the audience was very traumatized by it." Once the run was over, she never returned to it. "I'm not going to make an audience suffer for the sins still going on in the United States," she said. "I'm there as an entertainer. My job is to help people forget."

Deborah Pugh Remembers

As a volunteer for WriterCorps (an AmeriCorps project offering writing programs to women in homeless shelters and prisons), a white Southerner named Deborah Pugh worked with the largely black female inmates of the Washington, D.C., Correctional Treatment Facility. One night, they presented a show they'd organized for themselves. In I Have Arrived Before My Words: Autobiographical Writings of Homeless Women *(1997), Pugh writes that for one of the skits, several women put on white hoods and dragged a fellow inmate to a noose hanging from the basketball hoop. "After the mock lynching, another inmate sang Billie Holiday's 'Strange Fruit.' As the only white person out of a hundred or so*

*women, I did not feel frightened or guilty; mostly I felt
invisible. But a wash of sadness overcame me as I real-
ized how forcefully the meaning of this skit was festering
in these women's hearts. Always, as James Baldwin said,
history is upon our brows."*

～

The song had a profound impact upon Tori Amos when
she first heard it, in part because her grandfather was part
Cherokee and had grown up in the South—where, he
told her, European settlers had tried to wipe out anyone,
like his ancestors, with connections to the land. For
Amos, images like "blood at the root" were especially
powerful. Then there was that jarring juxtaposition: "He
takes you from one of the yummiest things—fruit—into
one of the darkest things: lynchings." "It would just ring
in my ears," she said of the song. "I just remember being
floored by it." She felt compelled to sing it, but first she
had to "put myself in a place where I wasn't normally,"
where her voice would be raw and she'd feel "completely
vulnerable." In the old adobe house in Taos that houses
her studio, she dragged herself out of bed at 5:30 one
morning and, without even a sip of water, went directly to
the piano and recorded it. Never, though, has she per-
formed it live. "I just can't walk into it," she said.

Natalie Merchant discovered "Strange Fruit" when she was fourteen years old and took out a Billie Holiday album from the public library in rural Westfield, New York. "Even as a teenager, I could tell that it was different," she said. Holiday's bravery led Merchant to write more political material, but never, she stressed, to do the song herself. "I sing it to myself because I love it, but I would never perform it live or record it," she said. "Some songs are best left to being interpreted by people who've really lived them and understand them." Nor has British pop singer Kate Bush recorded the song, but she did name a 1996 bronze sculpture, depicting Billie Holiday's mouth in midsong surrounded by flowers, *Strange Fruit*, which she has identified as one of her favorite Holiday numbers.

Karen Grigsby Bates Remembers

In 1995, Ward Connerly, a black member of the University of California's Board of Regents who opposes racial preferences, took umbrage when the Reverend Jesse Jackson described him as a "strange fruit." Four years later the song came up again, at least to one observer, during the Senate hearings over the impeachment of President Clinton. "It's a totally visceral reaction, but whenever I hear Trent Lott speak,

I immediately think of nooses decorating trees," Karen Grigsby Bates wrote in the Los Angeles Times, *referring to the Mississippian who is Senate Majority Leader.* "Trent Lott speaks and those nooses swing gently; Billie Holiday's 'Strange Fruit' is a muted soundtrack."

✎

Cassandra Wilson said that when she first heard "Strange Fruit" in her native Jackson, Mississippi, in the late 1970s, it "made my skin crawl." But many years passed before she felt she had the wisdom, the experience, the maturity, and the courage to tackle it. "That was a song that I always felt I had to get to," she said. "I had to reflect. I had to remember things about my past that I think I didn't want to look at. I had to talk to my mother and get a sense of that time and get a sense of her experiences." Her mother then recounted in great detail a lynching she had witnessed. What was part of the mother's memory became part of the daughter's, too.

Randomly but repeatedly, "Strange Fruit" kept coming up in conversations. "The material comes up to you and won't go away," Wilson said. "That's when you know that you have to deal with it, you have to confront it, you can't avoid it. What is it about this song that is saying 'Do me now!'? Believe me, that's not a tune that you want to do.

You want to hear it over and over again, but who's going to take on the responsibility of singing it? That's another thing altogether. I was afraid to record it, but I felt that I had to because of the feelings I have about the song and the importance of it. I think it's really important for us to revisit 'Strange Fruit.' "

One approaches the song, she said, not by trying to outdo or enhance Holiday, a fool's errand by any definition. Instead, Wilson stripped the song bare. Holiday sometimes performed "Strange Fruit" to punish an inattentive or unappreciative audience. But because the song is so emotionally taxing for her, Wilson sings it to reward audiences with whom she has established a special rapport. The races still react to it differently: blacks "have a conversation" with it, while whites approach it far more tentatively. There is still that interval of quiet afterward, that rest note before the applause.

Dee Dee Bridgewater first heard "Strange Fruit" while in her twenties; she, too, decided that it was something she could never do herself. "If a singer isn't ready to put herself on this emotional platter and just let herself be opened, it's a very frightening thing to undertake," she explained. But like Eartha Kitt, she portrayed Holiday in a one-woman show in the mid-1980s, and suddenly had no choice. Bridgewater subsequently included "Strange

Fruit" in her concert repertoire, but only when she felt she had a sufficiently sensitive pianist—a blind Dutchman named Bert van den Brink—accompanying her. Together, they performed it eight or nine times, always in Europe. Often, she cried as she sang it; sometimes, she choked on the ending. At least once, she could not finish.

She remembers best a concert in Turin, Italy. "There was just dead silence, then this amazing roar," she recalled. "In that deadness, I just broke down. I was sobbing. I had to leave the stage." Shortly after that, she decided never to sing it again. "I just can't do it anymore," she said. "I just don't want to go there."

But she has gone there, at least once. At an awards ceremony honoring Max Roach in Harlem in April 1999, she sang "Strange Fruit" a cappella—but only because Roach himself had requested it. "This is a song that is rarely sung today," she said, standing in a blackened room with a pinpoint of light upon her, just as Billie Holiday once did. "It is an important part of the history of our African-American music and our culture. It tells the story of a part of our past that is painful. But the story still needs to be told."

"Strange Fruit" Discography

THIS LISTING of recordings of "Strange Fruit" is from the 1998 OCLC Music Library and other resources. It may be incomplete.

Amasong
Over Here the Water Is Sweet
Ladyslipper Music, 1997

Tori Amos
Cornflake Girl (UK limited edition CD)
East West, 1994

Sidney Bechet
The Legendary Sidney Bechet
Bluebird, 1988

The Master Takes
Bluebird / Manufactured and distributed
by BMG Music, 1990

The Complete Sidney Bechet Vols. 3 and 4 (1941)
RCA, 1991

Terence Blanchard
The Billie Holiday Songbook
Columbia, 1994

Lester Bowie's Brass Fantasy
The Fire This Time
In and Out Records / Distributed by
Rounder Records Group, 1992

Dee Dee Bridgewater
In Montreux
Verve, 1991

Stan Campbell
Stan Campbell
Elektra, 1987

Fred Ho and the Afro-Asian Music Ensemble
The Underground Railroad to My Heart
Soul Note Records, 1994

Billie Holiday

The Best of Billie Holiday

Verve, 1972

Strange Fruit

Atlantic, 1972

Jazz at the Philharmonic:

The Historic Recordings (compilation)

Verve / Polydor Inc., 1976

All or Nothing at All

Verve, 1978

Fine and Mellow

Commodore, 1979

The Billie Holiday Songbook

Verve, 1985

Lady Day (1939–1944)

Commodore, 1988

(includes the April 20, 1939, session

that Columbia refused to record)

Compact Jazz Live!

Verve, 1990

Lady in Autumn: The Best of the Verve Years
(recorded 1946–1959) (two-disc box set) Verve, 1991
(includes live version from 1945 Jazz at the Philharmonic
concert at Los Angeles's Embassy Theater)

The Complete Billie Holiday on Verve 1945–1959
(ten-disc box set) Verve, 1992 disc 1: Jazz at the Philharmonic
concerts 1945–1947; Los Angeles studio session
disc 6: 1955 Los Angeles studio session;
1956 rehearsal at the Duftys' home
disc 7: 1956 New York and Los Angeles studio sessions

God Bless the Child
Pro Arte, 1992

Jazz at the Philharmonic
Verve, 1994

Jazz Legends (compilation)
RCA / BMG Direct, 1995

Lady Sings the Blues:
The Billie Holiday Story, Vol. 4
Verve, 1995

Billie's Blues
Magnum Music, 1996

Strange Fruit 1937–1939
Jazzterdays, 1996

Billie Holiday: The Complete Commodore Recordings
GRP Records, 1997

Ultimate Billie Holiday
Verve, 1997

The Jazz Singers (compilation)
Smithsonian Collection of Recordings
(Sony Music Special Products), 1998

Libby Holman
Libby Holman Sings Blues, Ballads, and Sin Songs 1954

Miki Howard
Miki Sings Billie: A Tribute to Billie Holiday
Giant / Reprise, 1993

Ranee Lee
Deep Song
Justin Time Records, 1990

Abbey Lincoln
Abbey Sings Billie Vol. 1
Enja, 1989

John Martyn
The Church with One Bell
Thirsty Ear Recordings, 1998

Carmen McRae
*Carmen McRae Sings "Lover Man" and Other Billie Holiday
Classics*
Columbia / Legacy, 1997

Marcus Miller
Tales
PRA Records, 1995

Live and More
PRA Records, 1997

Faith Nolan
Freedom to Love
Redwood Records, 1989

Lou Rawls
Black and Blue
Capitol, 1963

Diana Ross
Diana Ross Live: Stolen Moments
Motown, 1993

Lady Sings the Blues (soundtrack)
Motown, 1994

John Sellers
*Brother John Sellers Sings Big Boat up the River
and Other Blues and Folk Songs*
Monitor, 1958

Archie Shepp
Something to Live For
Timeless Records, 1997

Nina Simone
Nina Simone Sings Billie Holiday
Stroud, 1972

Don't Let Me Be Misunderstood
Mercury, 1988

Compact Jazz
Verve, 1989

Nina Simone
Mercury, 1989

Walkman Jazz
Polygram International Music, 1989

Pastel Blues / Let It All Out
Verve, 1990

Verve's Jazz Masters 17
Verve, 1994

Siouxsie and the Banshees
Through the Looking Glass
Geffen Records, 1987

Willie "the Lion" Smith
Lion and the Lamb
Topaz Jazz, 1996

Sounds of Blackness
Africa to America: The Journey of the Drum
Perspective Records / Manufactured and
distributed by A&M Records, 1994

Sting
*Conspiracy of Hope: Honouring Amnesty International's
25th Anniversary* (compilation)
Mercury, 1986

UB40
Signing Off
Virgin Records, 1980

Shirley Verrett
Singin' in the Storm
RCA Victor, 1966

Mal Waldron
For Lady (compilation)
Prestige Records, 1992

Catherine Wheel
Chrome
Phonogram / Distributed by
Polygram Records, 1993

Josh White
The Legendary Josh White
MCA Records, 1982

Sings the Blues and Sings: Vols. 1 & 2
Collectables Records, 1995

Josh White Jr. with Robin Batteau
Jazz, Ballads, & Blues
Rykodisc, 1986

Cassandra Wilson
New Moon Daughter
Blue Note / Manufactured by Capitol, 1995

Shirley Witherspoon
Where Do I Sign
NBS Listen, 1994

Robert Wyatt
Compilation
Gramavision / Distributed by Rhino, 1986

Nothing Can Stop Us
Thirsty Ear Recordings, 1998

Webster Young
For Lady (compilation)
Prestige Records, 1992

PHOTOGRAPHY CREDITS

1. Photograph by Mike Gould. © 1987 Delta Haze Corporation. All rights reserved. Used by permission.

2. Courtesy of *The New Yorker,* Conde Naste Publications, Inc. (*The New Yorker* March 1939)

3. Allen/Littlefield Collection, on deposit in the Special Collections Department, Robert W. Woodruff Library, Emory University.

4. Allen/Littlefield Collection, on deposit in the Special Collections Department, Robert W. Woodruff Library, Emory University.

5. © 1939 Time Inc., reprinted by permission.

6. Frank Driggs Collection.

7. Photograph by Charles Peterson, courtesy of Don Peterson.

8. Frank Driggs Collection.

9. Frank Driggs Collection.

10. Frank Driggs Collection.

11. Photograph by Charles Peterson, courtesy of Don Peterson.

12. Metronome/Bill Spilka/Archive Photos.

ABOUT THE AUTHOR

DAVID MARGOLICK is a contributing editor for *Vanity Fair*. Before that, he was a reporter for the *New York Times*. He is a graduate of the University of Michigan and Stanford Law School. He has written two prior books: *Undue Influence: The Epic Battle for the Johnson & Johnson Fortune* and *At the Bar: The Passions and Peccadillos of American Lawyers*, a collection of his law columns for the *New York Times*. *Strange Fruit* originated as an article in *Vanity Fair*.

ABOUT THE FOREWORD CONTRIBUTOR

HILTON ALS is a staff writer for *The New Yorker*. His first book, *The Women*, is out in paperback from Noonday Press.